R-3-E

MICH.

stern Ry.

Montreal R.

51

3 Veneer Co. R.R.

Pine L.

oose L.

C.&N.W. RY.

Roddis Lumber & Veneer Co. Railroad
and Dells & Northeastern Railway

DETAILED AREA

T-43-N

NG

Lake of
the Falls

Black

FF

MERCER

nd

lack

3rd Black L.

Little Turtle R.

ON
5

T-42-N

LE

N

FLAMBEAU

FLOWAGE

IRON

COUNTY

T-41-N

T-40-N

0 1 2 3 4 5   10

SCALE IN MILES

TYPICAL TOWNSHIP

6	5	4	3	2	SEC. 1
7	8	9	10	11	12
18	17	16	15	14	13
19	20	21	22	23	24
30	29	28	27	26	25
31	32	33	34	35	36

T-44-N

R-1-W

MAP BY - DONALD J. MOODY

R-3-E

the RODDIS
LINE

OVERLEAF

In a classic portrait of backwoods railroading, Roddis Lumber & Veneer Co.
No. 5, a Heisler, is shown proceeding cautiously over a spur track in Iron County,
Wisconsin. The year is 1937.

Wis. Natural Resources Dept.

the RODDIS LINE

The Roddis Lumber & Veneer Co. Railroad

and the Dells & Northeastern Railway

by HARVEY HUSTON

Published by Harvey Huston

860 Mount Pleasant, Winnetka, Illinois

Library of Congress Catalog Card Number: 78-184838
ISBN 0-9600048-2-3

For/O.N.H. and O.H.

TABLE OF CONTENTS

Introduction

This is primarily the story of a standard gauge railroad operated by Roddis Lumber & Veneer Company in northern Wisconsin. Built in 1903 to tap extensive hardwood forests in Ashland and Iron Counties, the "Roddis Line," as it was commonly known, was situated in the rolling country surrounding the headwaters of the Chippewa and the Flambeau, which were famous for white pine river drives in the nineteenth century. Originally a common carrier, the Roddis Line over the years became essentially a private railroad engaged in the transportation of forest products for the Roddis veneer and lumber mills at Marshfield and Park Falls. Forty-nine miles in length at the time of its abandonment in 1938, the Roddis Line was one of the last major middle western logging railroads.

The story also includes, somewhat as an epilogue, an account of the Dells & Northeastern Railway, the last common carrier railroad to be built in Wisconsin. The "Dells Line" was constructed in 1936 to reach hardwood forests in Iron County immediately to the northwest of the Roddis operations. Roddis Lumber & Veneer Company, which had abandoned its own logging railroad five years before, purchased the Dells Line in 1943 and operated it until abandonment in 1947, which was the final conclusion of Roddis' railroad operations.

This book, a mixture of railroad history and logging history, is intended to preserve the story of the utilization of these two railroads in the harvest of a great tract of hardwood timber, where abandonment of railroad operations coincided with exhaustion of a natural resource.

Historical Sketch

In 1890 Axel K. Hatteberg, superintendent of the Upham Manufacturing Co. furniture factory at Marshfield, in Wood County in central Wisconsin, developed a new veneer cutting machine which could handle a log ten feet long and four feet in diameter. With financial support from local citizens, The Hatteberg Veneer Co. was organized and a new plant opened in December, 1891. This factory utilized Hatteberg's cutting machine in producing hardwood veneer products, specializing in flour barrel headings and cheese boxes for the growing Wisconsin dairy products industry. After only two years of operations, The Hatteberg Veneer Co. encountered severe financial problems, apparently brought about by a shortage of capital and by the failure of a major customer which was heavily indebted to Hatteberg.

William Henry Roddis of Milwaukee entered the scene in March, 1894, by making an investment of $5,000 which enabled him to take control, and active direction, of The Hatteberg Veneer Co. Roddis, born in Troy, New York, on January 5, 1844, was brought at an early age to Milwaukee where his father, Thomas R. Roddis, a native of England, established a meat packing plant. W. H. Roddis, after his graduation from Milwaukee Academy, became a bookkeeper and cashier, and engaged in the real estate business until he moved to Marshfield.

W. H. Roddis presented a rather imposing appearance, regularly wearing a hard derby hat, frock coat, and striped trousers, and carrying a gold headed cane. He erected an equally imposing home on Fourth Avenue in Marshfield,

1

within easy walking distance of his business, which was renamed Roddis Veneer Company in 1897. He took an active interest in civic and church affairs, serving a term as Mayor of Marshfield, and for twenty-six years he was Senior Warden of St. Alban's Episcopal Church. He was a trustee of Nashotah House, a theological seminary at Nashotah, Wisconsin, and several times was a delegate to national conventions of his denomination. W. H. Roddis also had an absorbing interest in mathematics, attracting attention with his unusual ability to add columns of figures in his head with great rapidity.

Under W. H. Roddis' direction, the young veneer business prospered, and turned out such additional products as panels for folding beds, desks, pianos, and organs, while continuing its local monopoly in the production of cheese boxes. On April 20, 1897, the factory was destroyed by fire, but the setback was of short duration, for by July of that year the mill had been rebuilt and operations resumed. However, a more serious long range problem had developed, in that the nearby supplies of hardwood timber were becoming depleted. In fact, when the Roddis family moved from Milwaukee to Marshfield in 1894, Mrs. Roddis, a native of New Jersey, had exclaimed "There are more stumps than people!"

The Roddis mill had relied on oak and maple logs purchased locally in Wood County and in adjacent Marathon County but, as supplies became scarcer, Roddis was at a disadvantage in competing for the available timber with Upham Manufacturing Co. and with R. Connor Co. of nearby Stratford, both of which had their own logging railroads reaching into the forests.

It became essential to search elsewhere for a dependable supply of hardwood timber. The Wisconsin Central Railway, which had been completed between Stevens Point and Ashland in 1877, and which served the Roddis plant at Marshfield, was approached for a solution to the problem. In March, 1903, Roddis purchased from Wisconsin Realty Co., an affiliate of the railroad, a 36-acre site for a new mill on the Flambeau River at Park Falls in Price County, 95 miles north of Marshfield.

Price County and Ashland County, adjoining it to the north, had contained heavy stands of pine which, by the end of the nineteenth century, were substantially exhausted, particularly in the areas close to the driveable streams, of which the most prominent were the Chippewa and its major tributary, the Flambeau. In the area to the northeast of Park Falls, containing the headwaters of both the Chippewa and the Flambeau, there were, in 1903, scattered tracts of white pine not accessible to driving streams, plus vast quantities of hemlock and hardwoods, principally maple, oak, and birch, as well as white cedar (arbor vitae), balsam fir, and spruce. These timber resources were still largely untouched because hardwood logs would not float (nor would hemlock float easily, unless peeled and dried) and also because the lumber market provided a strong demand only for white pine. Thus the Park Falls region was especially attractive to a manufacturer of hardwood veneer seeking new sources of logs. The Wisconsin Central, on its part, was eager to have a new industry established which would make a substantial contribution to the railroad's thin traffic volume and which also would purchase large quantities of the hardwood timber growing on the railroad's extensive land grants.

Park Falls was not founded until several years after the Wisconsin Central was built. In the late 1880's the trains began to make regular stops at a location known as Muskelonge Falls where a small sawmill had been established. In 1890 the village of Muskelonge Falls (known as "Flambeau" on the railroad) was incorporated under the name of Park Falls.

Although the veneer plant at Marshfield used only hardwoods, the availability of large quantities of hemlock and white cedar, as well as lesser quantities of white and red pine, made it desirable for Roddis to build a sawmill, planing mill, and shingle mill at Park Falls, convenient to the timber, while the hardwood logs, or at least those of suitable veneer quality, would go to Marshfield, moving over the Wisconsin Central from Park Falls. In addition to constructing a plant, Roddis acquired standing timber, generally by outright purchase of the real estate and in other instances by purchase of timber rights, in an area to the northeast of Park Falls

3

which, ultimately, was about 25 miles long and 8 miles wide. These lands extended from Park Falls on the south to Island Lake in Iron County on the north, and were bounded generally on the east by the north fork of the Flambeau reaching upstream to the confluence of the Turtle and the Manitowish, and on the west by the east fork of the Chippewa.

In order to bring the logs to Park Falls, a railroad was necessary, and it was built by the Wisconsin Central. In September, 1903 construction was commenced on a standard gauge (4 ft. 8½ in.) line running 9½ miles in a northeasterly direction from the mill, following the west shore of the Flambeau and terminating at a location in Agenda Township in Ashland County. The *Park Falls Herald* pointed out that this was no mere logging railroad, that it was built for general freight and passenger traffic, that the Roddis company simply had trackage rights for its logging trains, and that the Wisconsin Central was considering a suitable depot site in the Agenda locality. Roddis and the Wisconsin Central had entered into a contract on June 15 whereby the carrier undertook to build 10 miles of railroad suitable for logging purposes with all extensions beyond the first 10 miles to be built by Roddis using rails furnished by the Wisconsin Central. In return Roddis agreed to pay all taxes on the railroad, and for a 20-year period to ship 8,000,000 feet of forest products outbound over the Wisconsin Central each year at full tariff rates, plus 500,000 feet per year for the eleventh and each additional mile constructed. The Wisconsin Central and its successor, Minneapolis, Saint Paul & Sault Sainte Marie Railroad (Soo Line) continued to supply Roddis with steel rails until the Roddis Line was abandoned thirty-five years later. In 1932 an on-the-ground inventory conducted jointly by Roddis and Soo Line personnel revealed that Soo Line rail was being used for 56 miles of Roddis trackage, including the main line, woods spurs, and the siding at the mill. At the termination of the Roddis railroad operations all of this rail was returned to the Soo.

George W. Campbell was transferred from Marshfield by Roddis as the first manager of the Park Falls mill, with responsibility also for the railroad and the woods operation. In addition to the mill, a blacksmith shop, warehouse, boarding house and horse barn were constructed. In recognition of the fact that the new mill would, for the first time, put Roddis into the business of manufacturing lumber, Roddis Veneer Company became Roddis Lumber & Veneer Company in September, 1903.

In October construction of the railroad was completed, and Fred Chabut, Park Falls street commissioner, described by the *Herald* as "one of the most capable woodsmen and river drivers in northern Wisconsin," was hired to take charge of Camp 1, near the north end of the new railroad. It was announced also that Mrs. Chabut would cook for the men in the camp, that 25 men had been hired and that more were needed. In November a side track was built between the Wisconsin Central main line and the mill, and the following month Roddis locomotive No. 1 was delivered and put to work. By January, 1904 the new mill was in operation with 50 employees, processing a large supply of logs which had been brought in over the new railroad. Locomotive No. 1 was delivering 10-car trains of logs three times each day.

The Wisconsin Railroad Appraisal of 1904 described the new Roddis Line as having 9.57 miles of main line and .78 miles of siding, with 60-pound rail, 24,846 softwood ties, no ballast, no fencing, 32,088 cubic yards of earthwork, 207 feet of pile bridges, 41,476 feet of culvert timber, 9 split switches with rigid frogs, 768 feet of crossing planks, 1 freight locomotive, 16 logging cars, and, at Park Falls, an engine house and coaling platform. The first annual report to the Railroad Commissioner, for the year ending June 30, 1905, of what was identified as the "Park Falls Spur of the Wisconsin Central Ry. operated by Roddis Lumber & Veneer Co." listed four railroad employees and their yearly compensation, consisting of one engineman at $960, one fireman at $540, one conductor at $660, and one section foreman at $525.

In its first full year of operations the Roddis Line transported more than 14,000 tons of logs, with the great majority of this traffic consisting of Roddis' own production. During the second year of operations the traffic volume increased to more than 17,000 tons of logs, and the Roddis Line underwent the first of a long series of extensions to tap additional sources of timber. By 1909 there were 15 miles of line, and at the time of the abandonment in 1938 this had grown to 49 miles.

Two years after the railroad commenced operations there were eight camps in the woods, employing about 425 men. One or two of these were company camps, operated directly by Roddis with its own foreman and crew at each, while the remainder were operated by "jobbers," who undertook to furnish a specified quantity of logs, managed their own camps and personnel, and loaded logs on to trains operated by Roddis crews. At that time it was customary to harvest timber seasonally, with the work concentrated in the winter, and woods activities were shut down for several months each year. In view of the limited season, it was necessary to employ a very large number of men in the woods to meet the company's log requirements.

1907 was a particularly difficult year for Roddis. Late in January extreme weather conditions closed the railroad for several days, resulting in a shutdown of the Park Falls mill when log supplies were exhausted. In the middle of February fire consumed the veneer plant at Marshfield, which had been rebuilt just ten years before, following an earlier fire. While the Roddis officials were giving consideration to abandonment of the Marshfield plant and transfer of all activities to Park Falls, a second fire, only eight days after the Marshfield fire, destroyed the Park Falls mill. With both mills burned to the ground, W. H. Roddis quickly reached a decision to rebuild at both locations. By May operations had been restored at Park Falls.

Prior to the outbreak of World War I in 1914, the Roddis Line had been pushed steadily northward through Ashland County to the Iron County line. Camps 3 and 4 were built along a new branch which joined the main line near Camp 1 and ran west for 4 miles to the Chippewa River. Beyond the Chippewa logging operations were conducted by Mellen Lumber Company, and the river became, for practical purposes, the western outpost of Roddis logging. By 1915 logging had been completed in the vicinity of Camp 1, and Camp 4 became the new woods headquarters. World War I stimulated a heavy demand for forest products, including the use of Roddis plywood for military aircraft, and by 1919 the Roddis Line was hauling more than 50,000 tons of freight each year.

6

1920 was a year of significant change for the Roddis Line. On November 6 W. H. Roddis passed away at the age of 76. The following month Hamilton Roddis, Treasurer of the corporation, succeeded his father as President of Roddis Lumber & Veneer Company.

Hamilton Roddis, born in Milwaukee on June 26, 1875, was a student at the University of Wisconsin Law School in April, 1897 when the Marshfield veneer mill burned down. H.R., as he was generally known, dropped out of school for a year in order to help his father restore operations at Marshfield. By studying nights and weekends he received his law degree in 1899 with his original class, and went to Spokane, Washington with the intent of practicing law there. In 1900 he returned to Marshfield and spent the remaining 60 years of his life working for Roddis Veneer Company and its successors. Like his father, H.R. took an active part in civic and religious affairs in Marshfield. 1920 also saw the departure of George W. Campbell, who had been manager for Roddis at Park Falls since 1903, and his replacement by E. H. Ruhmer.

In 1925 Roddis made a substantial change in its woods operations. Prior to that year most of the logging had been performed by crews directed by Roddis foremen and housed at Roddis camps, with a small part of the production handled by independent jobbers. But in 1925 Roddis turned over to Carl V. Nelson, a jobber, all of its woods operations with the exception of relatively insignificant production already being handled by small-scale jobbers. Until the termination of the arrangement in 1930, Nelson built and operated a total of ten camps and hired the loggers, with the railroad crews being the only Roddis employees involved directly in getting the timber out of the woods. Nelson also pursued the practice of year-around logging, which had been done previously by Roddis to a very limited extent. During the Nelson years two or three large camps, each employing about 125 men, were kept in operation simultaneously.

Early in 1925 the Chippewa & Flambeau Improvement Co. received authority from the Wisconsin Railroad Commission to construct a water storage reservoir and dam on the Flambeau River near the junction of the Turtle and Manitowish Rivers in Iron County. The location of the proposed

7

dam was approximately 8 miles southwest of Mercer and 5 miles to the east of the Roddis main line through Ashland County. Roddis held substantial timber acreage in the vicinity of the dam, including some lands which were to be inundated. Two years before, an alternate railroad main line had been built from North Line Junction, south of the original headquarters Camp 1, extending for 3 miles directly east to a new Camp 8 in Iron County. In 1925 this line was extended an additional 2 miles eastward to the site of the proposed Turtle Dam. This new main line provided access to several camps which Carl V. Nelson built within the next few years to the north and northwest of Turtle Dam, including his new headquarters Camp 1.

The Turtle Dam line extension also enabled Roddis to secure a contract to provide all necessary fill and to haul it to the dam site. Roddis used a large steam shovel to load earth into gondola cars, which one of the logging locomotives hauled to the dam, where a "Y" was built to turn the construction trains. By April 1, 1926 Turtle Dam had been completed, producing a reservoir area, variously known as the Flambeau Flowage or the Turtle-Flambeau Flowage, covering approximately 20,000 acres.

Construction of the dam and reservoir allegedly interfered with the annual spring logging drives of the Flambeau River Lumber Co., located approximately 100 miles downstream at Ladysmith. Litigation in the Circuit Court of Rusk County and before the Wisconsin Railroad Commission was resolved in 1928 by a Commission order directing the Chippewa & Flambeau Improvement Co. to release larger quantities of water in the early spring from Turtle Dam and from Rest Lake Dam, located upstream on the Manitowish. On the other hand, the new reservoir did not interfere particularly with Roddis' operations, for Roddis made little use of the Flambeau for log drives, with its last drive apparently having taken place in 1911 when quantities of cedar poles and pulpwood were driven downstream 13 miles to Park Falls. In addition to the contract to provide fill, Roddis received compensation of approximately $13,000 for flooding of its lands.

Not long after completion of the Turtle Dam project, Roddis abandoned most of its line extending eastward to C.

V. Nelson's Iron County camps, leaving in place a short spur at North Line Junction to serve as a "Y." The old main line was rebuilt to the north from old Camp 1, and logging was commenced in a portion of Iron County more than 20 miles from Park Falls. Nelson established a new woods headquarters at Camp 10 in Iron County, plus subsidiary camps 7, 8, and 9, each served by a logging spur track.

Operations under the Nelson contract were terminated in 1930, and Roddis again undertook to perform its own logging. John A. Morner was appointed manager at Park Falls, succeeding Grant Van Dusen, who held the position during most of the Nelson era. Roddis continued to use Nelson's Camp 10 as its own woods headquarters and, in 1930, built Camps 11 and 12 not far from Camp 10. In 1934 and 1935 Camps 14 and 15, respectively, were established farther north in Iron County, requiring construction of new trackage near Island Lake and Lake Six. Camp 10 remained as the principal railroad junction from which point trains to Park Falls were handled by main line locomotives which were too heavy to use on the spurs.

During the depression years of the 1930's there were frequent shutdowns of both woods operations and mill operations. By September, 1936 economic conditions had improved to the extent that electrification of the Park Falls mill was considered justifiable, and this work was carried out under the direction of the new Park Falls manager, Gordon R. Connor, a son-in-law of Hamilton Roddis. At the same time grading improvements were made on the railroad with the hope of reducing the risk of derailments.

Early in 1938 mill operations again were shut down, and all work was suspended at Camp 15, the last of the railroad camps. With the lumber and veneer markets depressed, and only a year's supply of timber available near Camp 15, there no longer appeared to be an economic justification for maintaining a railroad. After thirty-five years of operations, the Roddis railroad line was shut down, the track dismantled, and one of the last major middle western logging railroads was no longer in existence.

By December of 1938 production had been resumed at the Park Falls mill, but this time logs were brought in by

9

truck, and by rail only from Roddis-owned timber lands near Loretta, a point on the Chicago, St. Paul, Minneapolis & Omaha Railway in Sawyer County, west of Park Falls. In the winter of 1939-1940 Camp 15 was reopened and rehabilitated, having been damaged substantially by vandalism and thievery during the long period it had been unused. The remaining 8,000,000 feet of standing timber owned by Roddis in the vicinity of Camp 15 was cut that winter and hauled to Park Falls by a fleet of trucks, working day and night. The trucks used a road out of Camp 15, which was built by Roddis forces, and which extended to a connection with existing highways to Park Falls.

The close of the 1930's and the outbreak of World War II saw a revival of demand for forest products, and activities were at a high level at both Marshfield and Park Falls. In 1943, after a lapse of nearly five years, Roddis again was operating a logging railroad. On June 1 of that year Roddis purchased the Iron County timber lands and logging railroad of Dells Paper & Pulp Company. The timber, consisting principally of hardwoods and hemlock, was located close to Roddis' Island Lake properties, while the Dells railroad line, including both the common carrier Dells & Northeastern Railway and a connecting private logging railroad, came to within 1 mile of an old Roddis Line spur.

Since 1940 Roddis had been utilizing the Dells Line for transporting some of the logs cut in the vicinity of Roddis' new Camp 15, established that year 2 miles east of Lake Six. New Camp 15 was served exclusively by trucks, which hauled logs either to Park Falls or to a landing on the Dells Line via a truck road built by Roddis south and west of Island Lake. A branch from this road also provided access to Dells Line landings for jobber operations conducted by George A. Corrigan east of Island Lake.

The Dells Line acquisition enabled Roddis to use its logging railroad, rather than a long truck haul, for transportation to Park Falls via a Soo Line connection at Sells Spur in Ashland County. Logging in conjunction with the Dells Line was conducted not only in the Island Lake area but also on the timber lands acquired from Dells Paper & Pulp Company which extended northward toward the Penokee Range.

10

Early in 1947 the Dells Line was abandoned after all nearby timber had been cut and, once again, this time permanently, Roddis no longer owned a railroad.

Archie McClaire Collection

11

The veneer mill at Marshfield in 1900.
The water barrels on the roof could not save the plant from destruction
in the first of the disastrous fires of 1907.

Following the 1907 fire, the Marshfield plant was rebuilt and
enlarged substantially, as shown in this view during the 1940's.

An early view of the sawmill at Park Falls.

The Park Falls mill and "hot pond," around 1910.

From left to right are shown the two-stall engine house, office, and coal shed at Park Falls. The small appendage on the office building is the vault, to which manager George W. Campbell and the office staff fled for safety after Campbell had been wounded by a gunman in February, 1914.

A load of shingles from the mill is delivered locally in Park Falls. 1916.

The Park Falls mill in the early 1930's.

Exterior and interior (below, left) views of the Roddis boarding house
at Park Falls, circa 1908. Upstairs was a large room, known
as the "ram pasture," filled with bunk beds used by the lumberjacks
when they came to town. The gentleman wearing the derby
is the Roddis manager, George W. Campbell.

Standing in front of the blacksmith
shop at the Park Falls sawmill (right)
is William M. Martin, who was employed
by Roddis for many years successively
as section hand, section foreman,
fireman and engineer.

Frank Blanchard, teamster, with a load of finished lumber which
will be transferred to the Soo Line box car. Park Falls, 1916.

A 1916 view of the horse barn at the Park Falls sawmill.

Barns at the former Roddis farm, located on the old main line near the Flambeau River a short distance northeast of Park Falls. Many of the logging camp horses were kept here during the summers, when woods operations were less extensive than in the winter time. October 24, 1970.

William Henry Roddis, who guided the Roddis enterprises from 1894 until his death in 1920.

Hamilton Roddis relaxing at Butternut Lake, around 1912 or 1913. The Roddis family spent many summers at this lake, which was conveniently situated close to the Park Falls operations.

Hamilton Roddis, a proud young father, poses with his twin daughters, Mary and Sara.

Hamilton Roddis at his desk in Marshfield in 1955, just before his 80th birthday. At this time he had completed fifty-five years of service with the Roddis companies.

George W. Campbell, Roddis manager and the first automobile
owner in Park Falls, drives his 1908 Rambler touring car.
The vehicle was built at Kenosha by a predecessor of American
Motors, and transported to Park Falls via the Wisconsin
Central Railway from Burlington, Wisconsin.
The passengers are Chet and Bill Miller, Roddis bookkeepers,
and their three sisters. Campbell served as manager continuously
from 1903 to 1920.

John A. Morner, second from right, standing next to his daughter,
Ruth, at Camp 10, was Roddis manager at Park Falls from 1930 to 1936.

Railroad Operations

2

In December, 1903 the Roddis Line began operations with a single locomotive, No. 1, an American Standard (4-4-0 wheel arrangement) type. The source from which Roddis obtained this engine is not known, but presumably it had already seen considerable service elsewhere, for reports to the State of Wisconsin disclosed that while it was purchased for $2,592, its cost of reproduction was estimated at $5,332. No. 1 remained Roddis' only locomotive until 1911, when it was described as "worn out." In 1917 an ancient locomotive reportedly was supplying steam to the Park Falls sawmill—perhaps this was No. 1 at the end of its career.

For approximately its first ten years the Roddis Line used only one locomotive at a time. Woods spurs had not yet been built and all camps were located close to the main line, so rail operations were main line operations, with most of that main line consisting of the original 9½ miles built by the Wisconsin Central. Logging trains were short, and usually limited to ten cars. With short trains and a single locomotive it is understandable why logs were cut and piled on rollways faster than the trains could haul them to Park Falls.

During the World War I years Roddis woods operations became based on the simultaneous use of a headquarters camp and one or two satellite camps which were not necessarily located on the main line. This change in logging operations also meant a change in railroad operations. Henceforth, one or two engines stationed at Park Falls were assigned permanently to main line trains. Every morning such a locomotive took a train of empty cars out to the headquarters camp, bringing back in the late afternoon a train of loaded cars, followed by switching duties at the mill.

In 1923, after a line was built east from North Line Junction to Camp 8, there were, for practical purposes, two main lines, one going north to Camp 7 and the other east to Camp 8. Prior to this time, Engine No. 6, a large consolidation type, performed main line duties between Camp 7 and Park Falls. With the construction of the new line, No. 6 was reassigned to the Camp 8 line, while No. 7, a former Chicago, St. Paul, Minneapolis & Omaha passenger engine, worked between Camp 7 and the junction. There was a long siding at the junction, where empties were set out to be picked up by No. 7, and where No. 7 delivered loaded cars later in the day. A cabin was built at Camp 7 for Herb Hollinger, No. 7's regular engineer, and Mrs. Hollinger. No. 7 was treated as a personal pet by Hollinger, and a poem which he composed about this locomotive is set out in the Appendix.

After operations in the Camp 8-Turtle Dam area had been completed and a new woods headquarters established at Camp 10, the 28-mile line between this camp and Park Falls became the main line, with numerous spurs built in the vicinity of each camp. Track construction on the spurs was much less substantial than main line standards, for a typical spur remained in use for about a year before the rail was pulled and relaid elsewhere. Only the main line ties were squared, with the round ties on the spurs resembling pulpwood. Because of the light construction of the spurs, plus steeper grades and more curvature, the heavy main line locomotives were not used beyond Camp 10. The lighter woods engines brought their loads as far as Camp 10, where trains were made up for the long haul to Park Falls.

Throughout the 1920's and 1930's the Roddis Line, with the exception of Herb Hollinger's No. 7, used geared locomotives, rather than rod engines, in woods operations. In the early 1920's a Lima Shay and a Heisler were obtained, secondhand, for work on the spurs. In 1927 the Roddis Line acquired the only new engine it ever possessed, No. 10, a Heisler, while in 1930 an additional Lima Shay was purchased. While the Heislers were used extensively, the two Shays were worked sparingly, for apparently they were nearing the end of their

22

useful lives when obtained by Roddis. The Shay acquired in 1930 was sold to Roddis by Foster-Latimer Lumber Co. of Mellen, Wisconsin for $450; Mr. Latimer is reported to have remarked at the time that he sold the locomotive for the price of a used automobile.

By 1930 three geared locomotives, the two Heislers and the second Shay, were being used in the woods and a main line locomotive was bringing, six days per week, loads of 45 to 60 cars from Camp 10 to Park Falls, where cars of veneer logs were set out for the Soo Line to haul to Marshfield. For the Roddis Line's last few years Engine No. 4, a consolidation-type acquired from Flambeau River Lumber Co. of Lady-smith, and 2nd No. 7, a prairie-type obtained from Mellen Lumber Co. of Glidden, alternated in main line service.

Soo Line flat cars were used for carrying logs destined for Marshfield, while logs for Park Falls were carried on Roddis-owned flat cars or on Russell-type log cars, which were constructed without platforms, instead having bunks similar to logging sleighs. Cedar poles and railroad ties, and sometimes pulpwood, were carried in Soo Line box cars, with pulpwood also moving on flat cars or in gondola cars.

Supervisory personnel travelled over the railroad in automobiles equipped for rail operation, including a Chevrolet sedan and a Ford Model A coupe. There were also gasoline speeders for a variety of uses, including one fitted with an elaborate windshield for high-speed winter operations between the mill and the camps. Track maintenance was handled by two section crews, one stationed at Park Falls and the other at the headquarters camp.

The main line trains were each manned by an engineer, fireman and brakeman, while on the woods switching locomotives the crew consisted of an engineer and a combination brakeman-fireman.

Although, of course, wood was abundant, all of the Roddis Line engines burned coal. In addition to a bin at the mill, supplies were maintained at various camps, with the coal brought out from Park Falls in a specially constructed sheet steel car. Water supplies were obtained from wells at the camps and from creeks, including Deer Creek near old Camp 1, which was a regular source.

23

Most of the Russell cars were bought, used, from other logging railroads, although many were built at the Park Falls mill. The Roddis car supply apparently reached its peak in 1929, when the line had 82 Russell cars, 18 flat cars, 6 hog fuel cars, 4 ballast cars, and a caboose. Hog fuel (sawdust) from the mill was used as ballast in swampy locations.

Following the shutdown of the railroad in 1938, the leased rail was returned to the Soo Line and most of the railroad equipment was scrapped, although two or three of the locomotives were retained a few years to do switching at the mill. As far as can be ascertained, the only engine to survive for service elsewhere was 2nd No. 7, which is believed to have become No. 10 of the Dells & Northeastern Railway until abandonment of that line in 1947 when it, too, was scrapped.

Frank E. Salonen

Roddis train crews emerging from the woods had this view of the Park Falls mill. Winter, 1924-1925.

Martin Family Collection

Engine No. 1 with empty Russell log cars during the early years.

Engine No. 1 and crew stand by while loading is performed
by a Cody steam jammer. 1908.

STEAM LOADER

Another view of loading with a Cody jammer, with the logs held
in place with stakes, rather than chains.
The engine probably is No. 1 near the end of its career.

S. A. Johnson Photo, Martin Family Collection

No. 1 and a Cody jammer undertake a very substantial loading operation.
The time probably is shortly before World War I.
Standing, from left to right, are Engineer Mert Hayward,
Fireman Joe Corrigan, and Conductor-Brakeman Byron Mason.

Lester Blanchard Collection

Loading logs on the
main line in 1908.

Loaded Russell cars.
Note the private telephone line, built in 1911.

Empty Russell cars and a Soo box car on the
main line bisecting a desolate cutover area.

The main line in winter as seen from the top of the caboose, with a locomotive on the far horizon.

The original main line, a half-mile north of Whiteside's Crossing, and not far from Newell's Camp 2. August 19, 1970.

James P. Kaysen

The Chippewa River bridge on the line to Camp 6 as it appeared on October 24, 1970. The trackage was picked up in 1924 or 1925.

Locomotive No. 2 on a woods spur behind Camp 7. 1925.

Frank E. Salonen

Frank E. Salonen

Engineer Herb Hollinger, left, stands alongside
his favorite engine, 1st No. 7. 1925.

Posing in front of 1st No. 7 at Camp 5 in April, 1925, are
Engineer Herb Hollinger, left, unidentified in center,
and Fireman Jack Wood at right. A sharp eye will observe the number 68
(the number assigned to this engine when it belonged
to the Chicago, St. Paul, Minneapolis & Omaha)
on the headlight.

*Howard Peddle
Collection*

1st No. 7 with a train of loaded log cars near Camp 7, in 1925.

1st No. 7 waits with a train at North Line Junction
in the winter of 1925-1926.

A closer view of the same scene as in the preceding picture.
On the left, in the deep snow, is Carl V. Nelson, a jobber,
and next to him is Engineer Hollinger.

The first engine No. 7 is coupled to a Russell car and
the Roddis Line's only caboose on a fine summer day in 1925.

Frank E. Salonen

The steel gang working along the Turtle Dam line in 1925.

Engine No. 6 and train crew, around 1927, possibly
on the Turtle Dam line. Sitting on the front of the locomotive
is Engineer George Steiger, with Fireman Bill Martin
standing next to him. No. 6 proved to be too heavy for
satisfactory performance on the Roddis Line.

These two photos show the Roddis steam shovel removing earth
and depositing it on cars which would haul it to the site
of Turtle Dam for use as fill during the 1925 construction work.

Turtle Dam, on the Flambeau River, as it appeared during
the winter of 1925-1926. The dam was put into operation April 1, 1926.

Engine 1st No. 7 and speeder at Carl V. Nelson's Headquarters Camp 1 during
the winter of 1925-1926. Kneeling in front is Oscar M. Nelson, Carl's
brother, who served as foreman at several of the Nelson and Roddis camps.

Engine No. 10 at Nelson's Camp 1, about 1928.

The site of Nelson's Camp 1 as it appeared on the Fourth of July in 1970.

Looking northward at the site of Nelson's Camp 1 headquarters,
showing a telephone line paralleling the old railroad right of way.
An engine house and coal bin formerly stood at this location.
The building in the background is the Town of Mercer fire station,
facing Iron County Trunk Highway FF. July 4, 1970.

A view, in July, 1970, of a Roddis spur extending northward from
a point approximately one-fourth mile north of C. V. Nelson's Camp 2.

No. 5, one of the Heislers, switching on one of the Iron County
spurs in 1937. Jack Wood is the engineer.   *Wis. Natural Resources Dept.*

Wis. Natural Resources Dept.

Engine No. 5 and a speeder at a woods junction in Iron County.
Note how the ties, not being squared, closely resemble the pulpwood on the flat car. 1937.

No. 10 hauling pulpwood somewhere in Iron County, probably near one of the camps as the presence of a telephone line suggests. 1937.

George Steiger Collection

Engine No. 6 pulling a trainload
of logs during the winter of 1924-1925.
This is probably action on the main
line, even though the grade appears
rather steep.

Engine 2nd No. 7, with a long main line train headed for Park Falls,
pauses before crossing through a blueberry swamp which will be followed
immediately by a steep hill east of Camp 5.
This 1934 photo shows Brakeman Harry Sheedy on the ground,
with Engineer George Steiger and Fireman Bill Martin in the cab.

A 1937 photo of 2nd No. 7 on the main line hauling
a train of logs to the mill.

In 1925 Roddis supervisory personnel used this Chevrolet sedan
to travel over the railroad. The sawed-off brooms were
designed to remove snow and other obstructions from the rails.

The woods superintendent traveled over the line in this speeder, specially equipped for winter operation, as shown in this 1929 photo at Whiteside's Crossing.

The Roddis locomotives regularly took water from Deer Creek, north of Whiteside's Crossing, as No. 1 is doing here.

Henry S. Jones Photo,
Roddis Family
Collection
Dynamiting a swamp was a rather dramatic way of opening up a new
supply of water for locomotives and the camps. 1930.

Frank E. Salonen

Engine 1st No. 7 is shown here on an assignment, in 1925,
to haul water back to one of the camps.

Here the water tanks are being connected to a creek along the right of way.

A close-up view of the Roddis water car. The car was used for hauling water from rivers to the camps whenever well supplies were inadequate. The tanks supplied water to the steam jammers as well as the locomotives, and were kept filled for fire protection purposes.

The start of a new railroad grade; about 1925.

An aggressive porcupine occupies the main line. 1928.

Section gang with speeder. 1925, near Camp 8.

A Soo Line box car at Camp 7. Box cars were used for hauling supplies
to the camps, and outbound shipments of cedar posts, railroad ties,
and occasionally pulpwood. Soo Line flat cars hauled veneer logs
to Marshfield, as well as some pulpwood,
while Roddis-owned Russell cars carried logs to the Park Falls mill.

Veneer logs await shipment to Marshfield from Camp 7,
during the winter of 1924-1925.

On the left is the Camp 7 coal storage bin. Next to it is the coal car,
which had a body constructed of sheet steel with corrugated reinforced ends.

Woods Operations

CHAPTER 3

Since the Roddis Line was almost exclusively a logging railroad, particular attention should be paid to the gathering of the forest products which were transported by the railroad.

For roughly the first half of the Roddis Line's thirty-five years of existence, Roddis woods operations were conducted in close proximity to the railroad main line, and most of the woods work was performed in winter. Woods activities were directed by a woods superintendent, who maintained an office at whatever camp was then serving as woods headquarters, and also directed the work of the foremen in charge of the individual camps.

From the beginnings of its woods operations, Roddis relied in part upon independent logging contractors, known as "jobbers," who undertook to cut specified quantities of timber, belonging either to Roddis or to others, and deliver same to the railroad "landing" for loading. While some jobbers engaged in very limited operations, others established camps as large as the Roddis company-operated camps.

Ice roads extended into the timber from the camps along the railroad. After the right of way was cleared for such a road, a "rutter" was pulled by oxen or horses through the snow, making parallel grooves of the same gauge as the runners of the sleighs. During the colder night hours, wagons containing water tanks followed the path of the rutters, dripping water into the ruts. Wisconsin winter temperatures generally insured that by morning the grooves would be filled with ice, making a fixed track for the sleighs.

49

As the trees were felled, they were cut into lengths and skidded (dragged) by oxen or horses into clearings where, by means of various devices, they were loaded on to large sleighs. The sleighs, as loaded, were pulled by oxen or horses over the ice roads to landings along the railroad line. During the early years logs were brought in from the woods more rapidly than the short trains could haul them to Park Falls. Therefore, at the landings, instead of being loaded directly on to railroad cars, the logs were unloaded from the sleighs and piled high on "rollways" along the tracks. Whenever a train became available to move logs from a particular rollway, a steam powered crane, commonly called a "jammer," lifted logs off the rollway and on to railroad cars under the watchful eye of the "top loader," who had the responsibility of directing the jammer operator in the safe and efficient loading of each car.

Beginning about 1920 changes were occurring in Roddis' woods methods. Construction of feeder-type railroad spur tracks and the increasing practice of conducting all-year logging made the use of sleighs and ice roads relatively less important. As railroad spurs reached deep into the places where the timber was being cut, it was feasible to have horses skid the logs directly to the nearby tracks without resorting to sleigh hauls. With both steam jammers and locomotives operating simultaneously at various points on the Roddis Line, it was feasible also to load the logs directly on to the cars as they were skidded in from the woods, eliminating the need for temporary log storage on rollways.

Sleigh hauls were not entirely discontinued and, in fact, became more efficient. Instead of using animal power to pull sleighs, Roddis relied upon steam haulers to pull a train of sleighs along the ice roads. An internal combustion Holt tractor was also used for the same purpose.

A group of Roddis woods workers in front of a huge white pine just before the tree is cut. The two sawyers are at the left. 1926. ——

R. L. & V. Co.
Eau Claire Wis. 1926

Sawyers at work on the white pine shown in the preceding picture. The location was near Camp 7.

These photographs illustrate the size of the better timber available to Roddis near Camp 7 in the year 1925.

Sawyers with tree which they had just cut down.
Lying on the stump are wedges made of hard maple
or ironwood, dried and seasoned. Circa 1925.

Frank E. Salonen

Logs being skidded by C. V. Nelson's men with two-horse teams.
Winter, 1925-1926.

Oscar M. Nelson Collection

Sleigh loading operations in 1914. An A-frame loader is on the sled in front, with a tip-up loader in the rear.

Lumberjack using a two-horse team to skid a log out of the woods. About 1930.

This photo shows the loading of a sleigh with a swing boom loader.

A swing boom loader has just finished loading this sleigh
at Camp 5. Arthur LaBerge, the top loader, is second from the left.

A rutter at work cutting grooves on the ice road near Newell's
Camp 2 on the Chippewa River in 1916, following a heavy snowfall.
Bull puncher Dutch Pat stands beside the first ox team.

A water tank in use for icing a sleigh road.

Loaded sleighs and iced ruts at Newell's Camp 2, a short distance north of Whiteside's Crossing, about 1910.

Teamster McCarty stands next to a heavily loaded sleigh.
Large loads often were specially built up to please a photographer,
which may well have been the case here, for this would have been
a difficult hauling job for the single team of horses.

A sleigh haul in the winter of 1911-1912. Arthur LaBerge, an experienced
top loader, believes this is a genuine
operating load, rather than a staged scene.

Roddis Family Collection

Two photos of loaded sleighs at landings alongside
the railroad tracks. The second photograph shows the landing
at Charles Newell's Camp 6 in the winter of 1911-1912.

Frank Kleinsteiber Collection

S. A. Johnson Photo, Arthur LaBerge Collection

This use of a Holt tractor to haul a loaded sleigh at Camp 5
in 1920 constituted Roddis' first experiment with
internal combustion power to bring logs in from the woods.

Martin Family Collection

Steam haulers also were used to pull loaded sleighs.

Two early views of wintertime log decking along the Roddis Line.

Decking logs with a swing boom loader to await rail shipment to Park Falls. In the early years, particularly, the railroad could not handle the logs as fast as they were cut and decked.

S. A. Johnson Photo, Arthur LaBerge Collection

Decking logs at the Camp 4 landing, with loaded Russell cars
in the background. The suitcase was used by photographer Johnson
to carry his photographic equipment.

Louis Korth Collection

This photo, dating from about 1910, shows how the rollways
of decked logs were placed close to the railroad tracks.

Frank E. Salonen

A scene at Camp 7, in the winter of 1924-1925,
with fresh snow covering a quantity of logs which had been
unloaded from sleighs prior to rail shipment.

Frank Kleinsteiber Collection

This photograph, taken at Charles Newell's Camp 6
in Ashland County in the winter of 1911-1912, is said to include
4½ million board feet of decked logs.
More than 50 men also are shown. The man in the cutter
is believed to be Bill Drott, a Roddis foreman.

Ed Drott, Roddis woods superintendent, is ready with
his scale to measure a quantity of decked logs. 1916.

Frank E. Salonen

A log scaler, with his ever present yardstick,
at work near Camp 7.

A Cody jammer loading Russell cars near Newell's Camp 6 in 1911.
Charles Newell is standing on the ground next to the jammer.
The Russell cars were pulled through the jammer on the latter's own rails.

S. A. Johnson Photo, Frank Kleinsteiber Collection

A somewhat later photo of a Cody jammer loading a Russell car, with the logs held in place by stakes rather than by chains.

Loading a Russell car at Camp 5, with top loader LaBerge on the right of the log being held by the jammer cable.

A picture taking pause in the midst of loading pulpwood into a gondola car, about 1930.
Sitting in the center is August Reichert, the jammer operator.

A Cody jammer at Camp 8 during the early 1930's. This view illustrates how the jammer's rails were pulled back inside when loading operations were not being performed.

A Cody jammer on an Iron County spur, about 1930.

A slide jammer, which itself rested on a flat car,
is shown in 1926 loading logs on to a Soo Line flat car.

This load of veneer logs is destined for the mill at Marshfield.
Leaning against the logs is August Hatfield,
the top loader who was responsible for placing the logs
so as to insure proper balance and density. Circa 1925.

Hardwood logs and hemlock pulpwood await truck loading at New Camp 15, established near Lake Six in 1940, two years after abandonment of the Roddis railroad.

The Logging Camps

CHAPTER 4

The center of woods operations was the headquarters camp, where the woods superintendent maintained his office. The first Roddis headquarters camp was, appropriately, Camp 1, which was established in 1903 along the main line in Ashland County about 3 miles north of County Trunk Highway F. The highway crossing was generally referred to as Whiteside's Crossing, by reason of the fact that about one-fourth mile to the west there stood (and still stands today) the imposing farm house of William Whiteside. Much of the land in the vicinity belonged to Whiteside, who raised fine trotting horses and also prospected locally for iron ore. Fred Chabut, who was to operate camps for Roddis for more than twenty years, became the first foreman of Camp 1, while Bill McDonald was appointed woods superintendent.

Various jobbers' camps were established as early as 1904 near Camp 1, but these apparently were of little significance. However, two large jobber camps, designated Camp 2 and Camp 6, were established about 1906 by Charles Newell of Butternut between Camp 1 and Whiteside's Crossing.

Each of the camps operated by Roddis typically contained housing for a crew of about 125 men, including sawyers and loaders, as well as such specialists as a barn boss, cook and cookees (cook's helpers), blacksmith, saw filer, camp clerk, log scaler, and jammer operator. Buildings usually included one or two bunk houses, a cook shanty, an office, a blacksmith shop, a filing shack, a horse barn, pig pens, a small store known as a "wanigan," and perhaps an engine house and coal bin. In 1911 Roddis built a private telephone

69

system connecting Park Falls with the camps, and this greatly facilitated the close liaison necessary to insure a dependable flow of logs to the mills. By 1930, using speeders and automobiles equipped with railroad wheels, Roddis was able to boast of twice-daily mail service to the camps. Subsequently Hamilton Roddis supplied each camp with a battery-powered radio so that the men would not have to depend on day-old newspapers brought from Park Falls by the morning train as their source of news.

Camp 1 served as the first headquarters camp for about ten years. In 1914 Camp 4, located on the Chippewa River at the end of a 4-mile branch line running west from Camp 1, became the headquarters, with Bill Drott as foreman and his brother, Ed, as woods superintendent. Camp 3, with Fred Chabut as foreman, was established half-way between Camps 1 and 4. Charles Newell, who had finished his jobber operations at his Camps 2 and 6 along the original main line, built, in 1915, a new Camp 2 on the east shore of the Chippewa about one mile northeast of Camp 4. No railroad track was ever built to Camp 2; instead, an ice road was carved out on the west bank of the Chippewa extending downstream to Camp 4, where the logs were loaded on the railroad. After Newell had operated this Camp 2 for about a year, the Roddis company took over its control; Fred Chabut served there as foreman until the camp was closed in 1921.

Not long after construction of the Chippewa River extension to Camp 4, the original main line was extended northward into Iron County. By this time Roddis owned 28,000 acres of timberlands in Ashland and Iron Counties. Camp 5 was built just north of the county line, and from that point a 2-mile extension of the railroad was constructed north and west across the Chippewa to Camp 6 at Silver Creek.

In the early 1920's the principal logging was done in the vicinity of Camps 5 and 6, with John McDonald holding the position of woods superintendent, Fred Chabut foreman of Camp 5, and Adam Grosbier foreman of Camp 6. In 1923 a large new camp, No. 7, was established in Iron County about 2½ miles northeast of Camp 6 and about 3 miles north of Camp 5, with which it was connected by an extension of the railroad. Operations gradually were terminated at Camps 5 and 6, while Camp 7 remained active until 1925, with Angus McDonald, Fred Chabut, Paul Lytle, and Elmer Foster serving as foreman in rapid succession. John McDonald was succeeded as woods superintendent in 1923 by John Lucas, who in turn was succeeded the following year by Otto Heinski.

At approximately the same time Camp 7 was opened, Roddis determined to exploit additional resources to the east near the juncture of the Turtle and the Manitowish Rivers. From a point a short distance south of the old Camp 1 headquarters, the Roddis Line was extended due east for 3 miles to a new Camp 8 in Iron County.

As related in the opening chapter, 1925 was a year of changes in the Roddis woods activities. Logging was concluded in the Camp 5 - Camp 6 - Camp 7 area and concentrated in newly tapped locations in the vicinity of Camp 8. In addition, with the exception of certain minor jobbing work, all Roddis woods operations were contracted to Carl V. Nelson, as sole jobber, in lieu of Roddis handling directly its own woods work.

Forking to the north from the 1925 line extension to the site of Turtle Dam, a railroad line was built to Nelson's new headquarters Camp about 1 mile north of Camp 8 and close to what is now designated as Iron County Trunk Highway FF. During the next two years Nelson built his Camps 2 through 6 along new trackage north and northeast of his headquarters Camp 1, where he built an engine house and coal shed. Joe Ledvina was Nelson's foreman at Camp 1, Harry Sheedy at Camp 2, Mandus Hultquist at Camp 3, Oscar M. Nelson (Carl's brother) at Camp 5, and Herman Ihlenfeldt at Camp 6, while Camp 4 was operated by another jobber. Nelson operated three camps at all times, with crews totalling 400 men, plus 35 teams of horses, and year-around operations.

In 1927, with logging completed in the Turtle Dam region, Roddis built a new main line extending northeast from the original line, from which it branched off near old Camp 1, and ran to a point in Iron County about 1½ miles east of old Camp 7; here Nelson established Camp 10, his new headquarters. Spurs from the new railroad line were built to Nelson's Camps 7 and 8 in Ashland County, and to Camp 9 in Iron County, due east of the old Roddis Camp 5. Oscar M. Nelson served as foreman successively at Camps 7 and 8.

The Nelson jobbing contract was terminated in 1930. Roddis appointed John A. Morner manager at Park Falls and Gust Carlson woods superintendent. Roddis continued the use of Camp 10 as woods headquarters. Between 1930 and 1934 Roddis opened Camp 11, 2 miles northwest of Camp 10, Camp 12, about 1½ miles southeast of Camp 10, and Camp 14, near Lake Six and about 3 miles northeast of Camp 10. Camp 11 also featured a 3-mile ice road to reach an 80-acre tract of timber which was too isolated to justify construction of a railroad spur. Oscar M. Nelson was foreman at each of these three camps, being succeeded as Camp 12 foreman by Oscar Barnhardt when Nelson moved to Camp 14. The failure to designate a camp as No. 13 was, understandably, deliberate. As had been the practice in the areas logged by Carl Nelson, many spurs were built in the vicinity of Camps 11, 12 and 14.

In 1935 Roddis built the last of its railroad-served camps, which was located about 3 miles east of Camp 10. It was designated Camp 15, with Mike Laveck and Charles Nelson, successively, serving as foreman. By 1937 operations had been concluded at Camps 11, 12 and 14, leaving Camp 15 as the only active camp. Railroad service was continued, via Camp 10, to Camp 15 until the line was abandoned in 1938.

The work of log scalers, pulpwood checkers, and camp clerks was particularly exacting. Sawyers and loaders, sometimes referred to as piece workers, received payment for logs and poles on a per foot basis, while pulpwood, hemlock, spruce, balsam and cedar were paid for on a per cord basis. The crew who laid rails were known as the "steel gang" and were paid on the basis of "stations" (100 ft. segments) completed. The work of the log scalers and the pulpwood checkers not only determined the compensation of large numbers of men, but also provided the mills with advance estimates of the quantities of forest products they could expect to receive. In maintaining the camp books, the camp clerk made out the monthly payroll, keeping the time of the personnel paid on a monthly basis, and posting the work of the piece workers; he also checked the data of the scalers, pulp checkers and jobber checkers as to the timber cut, loaded, and sent to the mills, ordered camp supplies for the wanigan, cook shanty, horse barn, hog pens, blacksmith, and filer, as well as coal and repair parts for locomotive and jammer, checked in incoming and outgoing personnel, and kept records of meals of piece workers, monthly paid personnel, and transients.

During the entire period the Roddis Line was in service there were scattered small-scale jobbing operations. Individuals or small groups of men, including farmers supplementing their income with woods work during the winter, produced pulpwood or cedar lagging, and assumed the responsibility of delivering these products to landings along the railroad. These activities usually were directed from isolated forest shacks not grand enough to be referred to as logging camps.

Work in the woods carried considerable risk. Riding sleighs on downhill slopes could be especially hazardous. The *Herald* expressed anxiety, in March of 1907, when Emil Wepfer, a prominent member of the Park Falls baseball team, was injured while working at Newell's Camp 6 when a log slipped on a sleigh going down a grade, throwing Wepfer between the horses; Wepfer was able to return to work some weeks later and, hopefully, was able to play baseball again, too. Upon another occasion major surgery was required to save the life of a camp barn boss who had been kicked by a horse. Dead branches knocked loose by the impact of a falling tree were particularly dangerous and, for good reason, were called "widowmakers."

Many of the lumberjacks invested in "hospital tickets," providing for hospitalization in return for a fixed fee. Hospitals in Ashland and Chippewa Falls offered such arrangements, and salesmen representing each hospital regularly made the rounds of the camps soliciting purchases of tickets.

Although each camp represented, in population, the equivalent of a small village, today few traces remain of the camps along the Roddis Line. When a camp was shut down, all buildings were destroyed or moved in order to eliminate a fire hazard. Consequently, only a large clearing in the forest now typically marks the location of one of the Roddis camps.

The Camp 1 workers pose for a group picture, around 1913.

The Camp 1 teams and teamsters, shown outside the barn in 1913, performed a vital role in transporting the logs out of the woods.

James P. Kaysen, author of "The Railroads of Wisconsin, 1827-1937," and Arthur LaBerge, who went to work for Roddis as a top loader in 1913, visit the site of Roddis' headquarters Camp 1 on October 24, 1970.

Group at Charles Newell's Camp 6 in 1913. Charles Newell and his brother, Roy, are at left in the back row, while Mrs. Newell is in the second row next to the teamster, Dutch Pat, and the Newell children sit in front. The huge dinner horn is held by the cookee.

Two views of Camp 2 on the Chippewa River, dating from the winter of 1915-1916. The group scene includes foreman Fred Chabut at left in the top row, top loader Arthur LaBerge third from left in the second row, and a full complement of camp dogs.

S. A. Johnson Photo,
Arthur LaBerge Collection

Sleigh loading operations at Camp 2
on the Chippewa River are directed by top loader
Arthur LaBerge from the top log.

Harvey Huston

Arthur LaBerge at the Camp 2 loading point
in October, 1970, more than a half century
after the preceding picture was made.

Although Camp 2 was shut down in 1921, its horse barn was still more or less intact on October 24, 1970.

The site of Roddis Camp 3 as it appeared in 1970.

Camp 4, at the end of a 4-mile branch line
running west to the Chippewa River, replaced Camp 1
as the Roddis headquarters camp.

A steam jammer at work at the Camp 4 log landing.
Cedar poles are stacked in the foreground, and a few camp buildings
can be glimpsed beyond the trees in the background.

Frank E. Salonen

Cutting firewood at Camp 5 in 1924.

The location of Camp 5 as it appeared in 1970.

Harvey Huston

Summer and winter views of Camp 7, as it appeared in 1924 or 1925.
In the winter scene the center building is the cook shanty, which
is flanked by two bunkhouses. The two smaller buildings to the right
were used for food storage. The "bull cook," a sort of camp janitor,
is standing on the flat car which holds the water storage tanks.

The Camp 7 barn boss feeds the horses.
He was also responsible for feeding the camp's pigs.

The barn boss is shown in front
of the Camp 7 blacksmith shop
in the winter of 1924-1925.
The small building in the center
is the filing shack, and at the
right is the camp office.

John Lucas, woods superintendent,
and two cooks from Camp 7 pose with
the dinner horn in 1924.

This cabin was the home of locomotive engineer and
Mrs. Herb Hollinger at Camp 7 in the winter of 1924-1925.
Hollinger was assigned to engine 1st No. 7, which
worked regularly between Camp 7 and North Line Junction.

Frank Salonen, the youthful clerk at Camp 7, is shown
checking loading operations in 1925.
In addition to handling the heavy schedule of chores
assigned to a camp clerk, he found the time to make
an excellent photographic record of a great variety
of Roddis' railroad and logging operations.

A panoramic view of Camp 7 during the winter of 1924-1925.

Carl V. Nelson's Camp 1 in Iron County, in 1926.
This camp served as the first of Nelson's headquarters camps
during the period when he held a contract
to perform all of the logging operations for Roddis.

Carl V. Nelson is third from the right in this 1926
photograph taken at his Camp 1 headquarters.
Third and fourth from left are Ed Kelly and Joe Ledvina,
cook and foreman, respectively, of Camp 1.

Personnel of Nelson's Camp 1 in 1926. The locomotive is probably 1st No. 7.

Their important status justified this separate group portrait
of the horses and teamsters at Nelson's Camp 1.
At the right are C. V. Nelson and Nels, the filer, who was obviously
interrupted in his work when asked to pose.

Deep snow has almost hidden the railroad tracks in this 1926 scene
at Nelson's Camp 2 in Mercer Township, Iron County.

Oscar M. Nelson Collection

Part of the crew at Nelson's Camp 3 in Iron County during the winter of 1925-1926. One member of the group, it will be observed, continued to read a Minneapolis newspaper as the photograph was being taken.

Ruth Morner Collection

Camp 10 was built by C. V. Nelson as his second headquarters camp. It is shown here in the early 1930's after the Roddis company resumed handling its own logging operations and retained Camp 10 as the woods headquarters.

Camp 14, built in the early 1930's near Lake Six, was the next-to-last of the Roddis camps served by the railroad.

A saw filing shack was considered an indispensable part of each camp.

A saw filer at work in the woods. 1930.

Typical Roddis dining facilities, probably at Camp 10.

S. A. Johnson

Dinner at the Camp 4 landing on the Chippewa during
the winter of 1915-1916. The meal was prepared by the women cooks
in the tent, but it was consumed outdoors regardless of temperatures.
Art LaBerge, third from left in the front row, recalls that it was necessary
to finish up a plate of baked beans quickly before they could freeze.

Frank E. Salonen

This dinner was cooked at the camp, then brought
by sleigh to the location where the men were working. 1925.

Lumberjacks relax along the railroad tracks after finishing their noon dinner.

Jerome W. Best Collection

When a camp was closed permanently, the larger buildings were
dismantled and burned, but it was possible, as shown here,
to have smaller buildings hoisted by a jammer
on to railroad cars and moved to new camp locations.

Scattered throughout the Roddis woods operations were the small scale
activities of certain pulpwood jobbers,
often employing only the members of an immediate family.

Frank E. Salonen This picture shows a group at their cabin in the winter of 1924-1925.

Business Notes

5

Although the Roddis Line was operated as an integral part of Roddis Lumber and Veneer Company, annual reports as a railroad were filed from 1905 through 1932 with the Wisconsin Railroad Commissioner and the successor Railroad Commission and Public Service Commission, and in so doing, it must have appeared necessary to the Roddis management to attempt some sort of separate railroad financial reporting. The technique used was to report the cost of railroad operations for the year, and the revenue received from hauling non-proprietary freight (i.e., where Roddis was not the shipper); the difference between the total operating expense and the revenues from the non-proprietary traffic was assigned arbitrarily as revenue from Roddis' own traffic. In this manner operating revenues invariably equalled operating expenses.

Reported freight revenues from outside business ranged from a low of $123.50 for 1907 to a high of $3,008.75 in 1911, except for 1925 when outside revenues were shown as $7,-192.51. Presumably this record sum represented receipts pursuant to the Turtle Dam contract. After 1925 Roddis reported only operating expenses to the State, making no attempt to segregate non-company material if, indeed, Roddis hauled such traffic after that date.

Practically all traffic transported on the Roddis Line consisted of forest products, described variously as logs, slabs, shavings, pulpwood, cedar posts, poles, piling, ties, and bark, with the principal exception being the earth fill for Turtle Dam. While Roddis reported specifically that the railroad received freight "from farmers and others living along the right of way," it is not known whether any of this traffic consisted of potatoes, hay, or livestock, items often handled by other northern Wisconsin logging railroads. Although numerous passengers were carried by the Roddis Line, no tickets were sold; a typical report to the State revealed that "if any passengers go over this spur, they are carried without charge."

At the time of the original construction of the Roddis Line in 1903, it was the general impression that the railroad would be operated as a common carrier and not as a private line. In 1906 the Railroad Commission received an informal complaint from Winnebago Realty Co. alleging that Roddis had refused to transport the complainant's forest products over the railroad. The matter was settled by correspondence, with Roddis agreeing to publish a rate and to carry the complainant's freight. The following year Roddis Lumber & Veneer Company applied to the Railroad Commission for authority to discontinue operations as a common carrier. The Commission's annual report for 1908 indicated the status of this application as follows:

> "The above named company operates a railroad twelve miles long, running in a northwesterly (sic) direction from Park Falls into Ashland County. It was constructed for the purpose of hauling certain forest products from the lands which the above named company owned in the section through which the railroad runs. Their total gross earnings for the year ending December 31, 1906 amounted to but $354. In the above entitled matter they applied to the Commission for authority to discontinue business as a common carrier. The matter was taken under advisement and no action thereon has ever been taken, nor has the company asked anything further relating to it."

Files of the Public Service Commission disclose that the last tariff filing by Roddis was in 1906, and that in 1911 the Railroad Commission concluded that the Roddis Line was not a common carrier. Nevertheless it was not until 1934 that the State Tax Commission also concluded that the railroad was not a common carrier, and as late as 1936 the Public Service Commission answered an inquiry from Heineman Lumber Co. of Merrill by advising that the Roddis Line "was at one time operated as a common carrier, but it has not been so operated in recent years."

The Roddis enterprise increased substantially in size over the years, although there were setbacks during the intermittent periods of weak demand for forest products, with such setbacks reflected in periodic shutdowns of both woods operations and the Park Falls mill. One such low point was in 1908, but in October of that year the *Herald* predicted confidently that Roddis "will have a large number of men in the woods this winter if times pick up after election, as times undoubtedly will pick up in the event of the election of Taft and a Republican Congress." A few months later the *Herald* noted with satisfaction that Roddis' winter cut of logs had been larger that that of the previous year, so apparently times had indeed picked up with the election of President Taft.

Demand for forest products rose dramatically during World War I, by which time the Marshfield veneer plant was concentrating on production of plywood rather than cheese boxes and other specialty products. During the decade of the 1920's the demand for plywood and for finished lumber insured a high level of activity in the woods, with production averaging approximately 10,000,000 feet of forest products per year.

The 1930's decade, including a severe economic depression, resulted in a sharply reduced demand for lumber and plywood, with various mill and woods operations discontinued for months at a time. News of even limited, and short lived, resumption of operations was given wide publicity. In February, 1932 the *Herald* announced that Roddis had hired sixteen men to cut pulpwood and was looking for thirty-four more; the pay offered was $1.75 per cord for 4-foot cord wood, with camp board furnished at 18¢ per day, and the company supplied a horse to drag the wood to the tracks.

In November of that year a substantial reduction in the assessed valuation of the Park Falls plant was obtained. Hamilton Roddis, in a letter published in the *Herald*, explained why the company sought adjustment of its taxes,

95

pointing out that the machinery at Park Falls had been obtained second-hand in 1903 at a cost of $2,500 from a plant at Arpin in Wood County, and that the Park Falls plant had lost substantial sums of money in recent years. The letter added:

> "We are making every effort to pay expenses and to give our people employment. In this effort we confidently look for the cooperation of the citizens of Park Falls and their assistance, because their attitude and the attitude of the public officials must govern very largely the policy of this company in regard to future operation at Park Falls."

Roddis Lumber & Veneer Company, in the face of substantial difficulties, managed to survive the depression years of the 1930's. In addition to the periodic shutdowns of operations, the Park Falls office was closed in 1931 as an economy measure, with office duties and personnel, other than John A. Morner, the manager, transferred to Marshfield.

In August, 1933 Roddis put into effect a new scale of wages and hours in accordance with the lumber industry code instituted by the National Recovery Administration, known as the NRA. This produced a 40-hour week and 30¢ per hour minimum wage at the mill and, in woods work, considered a seasonal occupation, a 48-hour week and 27¢ per hour minimum wage.

The sawmill was closed down continuously from April to December, 1938, when, after an overhaul, it was reopened with preference in employment given to the men last in service with the company, but meanwhile the railroad had been shut down permanently.

Demand for forest products improved markedly during World War II, and the Marshfield plant produced large quantities of marine interior woodwork for the Liberty and Victory classes of merchant ships. Although the Roddis Line was abandoned in 1938, logs were brought to Park Falls by truck as well as by rail from other areas, including, between 1943 and 1947, rail shipments from landings on the Roddis-owned Dells & Northeastern Railway. Following abandonment of the Dells Line in 1947, the mill at Park Falls was

96

converted to produce pulp from popple (aspen) which grew rapidly on the cutover lands. In 1956, after Roddis sold the cutover lands which had been served by the Roddis Line and the Dells Line, the Park Falls plant again was converted, this time to a limited operation producing slabs for solid core doors. That work is still being performed at Park Falls, and the doors are completed at Marshfield.

As the impact of the depression lessened, Roddis undertook a course of great expansion, building or acquiring large plants at Ironwood, Michigan, Sault Sainte Marie, Ontario, Princeville, Quebec, and, subsequently, at Arcata, California, where extensive Douglas fir timber lands were acquired. Roddis Lumber & Veneer Company became Roddis Plywood Corporation in 1948, and in 1951 a first public offering of Roddis Plywood stock was marketed.

On March 27, 1960 the long career of Hamilton Roddis terminated with his death in Marshfield. Still Chairman of Roddis Plywood Corporation, he had watched the small Hatteberg Veneer Company grow into a group of enterprises with sales exceeding $59,000,000 per year, and more than 3,500 employees in the United States and Canada. Four months later, on August 1, 1960, Roddis Plywood Corporation was merged into Weyerhaeuser Company of Tacoma, Washington, thereby providing Weyerhaeuser with an entry into the manufacture of hardwood plywood.

Misfortunes...& Pleasures

CHAPTER **6**

Over the years the Roddis Line and the mills were subjected to a variety of obstacles. Not the least was the danger of fire.

As mentioned previously, the Marshfield veneer mill burned down in 1897, and within an eight-day period in 1907 fire destroyed both Marshfield and Park Falls mills. Fire struck the Park Falls plant again in January, 1928, but quick action by the local volunteer fire department prevented serious loss, prompting a financial contribution from a grateful Hamilton Roddis. Forest fires, sometimes caused by steam locomotives and sometimes by farmers clearing land or by careless berry pickers, were especially alarming because it was impossible to obtain insurance on standing timber. There was a very heavy loss from a forest fire in May, 1909 near Newell's Camp 2, while smaller losses were incurred on several other occasions. Whenever use of a camp was terminated, all buildings which were too large to be moved to a new location were burned so that the lumber would not be available as fuel for a future forest fire.

The cruel northern Wisconsin winters sometimes presented difficult problems for the Roddis Line, especially when a heavy blizzard was followed by a siege of below zero temperatures. In January and February, 1907, a combination of deep snow and several nights of temperatures as low as 39° below zero stopped all railroad operations. The Park Falls mill soon ran out of logs, and was forced to shut down for several days at the very peak of its seasonal operations.

Again, in 1914, heavy snow marooned the camps, and it required nine days of shoveling by the section hands to open

99

up 15 miles of track. In the meantime, the camps almost ran out of food, and, as the snow shovelers worked their way into the woods, they met many loggers who had started the long walk to Park Falls on the right of way. Snow blocked the line again during the last winter of operation, in 1937. It took the combined force of engine nos. 4, 5, and 10 behind a snowplow to open up the line to the camps, where only the tops of buildings were visible, and the loggers had built snow tunnels to trackside.

Early in 1907, in a complaint filed with the Wisconsin Railroad Commission, it was alleged that at a grade crossing near the south end of Ashland County it was the practice of the Roddis section gang to remove the crossing planks each autumn and not to replace them until the following spring. After receiving oral testimony from the complainant, and an affidavit from Roddis declaring that the planks were removed to permit passage of a locomotive and snowplow and immediately thereafter replaced, the Commission issued an order directing improvements to be made at the crossing, and included the comment that:

> *"It is no doubt easier to tear up the planks during the winter season when snow plowing must be resorted to, than it is to stop at each crossing and so adjust the flasher as to enable the engine to pass safely over the crossing, but this would hardly justify tearing up all the crossings in the state and leaving them torn up during the winter season."*

Train wrecks were not infrequent. In operating over a hilly terrain, it was customary for the locomotive engineers to get up steam to top the up grades, which of course made it necessary to buck the momentum of the down grade on the other side, a difficult feat since there were no brakes on the Russell-type log cars. On one memorable occasion in 1937, a short distance from Camp 10, a train of 40 to 45 cars of logs broke apart going down hill and broke apart a second time going up the next hill, with the sad result that the cars still going down the first hill met the cars falling back from the second hill. Logs and cars were scattered everywhere and, understandably, putting things back together was not easy.

100

Livestock in the farming region near Park Falls through which the railroad passed could also be a hazard, and an entire string of empties was derailed on one occasion when the train struck a group of calves. It was rare, however, when a railroad employee was injured. The only such injury reported to the State occurred in 1914 when:

"One car jumped the track and our conductor was thrown out—his head struck stump. He was laid up for 2½ months (about)—we paid him 65% of his wages and his doctor's bill."

A narrow escape was described dramatically by the *Herald* of March 1, 1935:

"Wednesday morning Edwin Schultz had a close call. As he has done hundreds of times before, he attempted to board the front end of the caboose of a train to ride to the Roddis mill where he is employed. The train was moving at about 10 to 15 miles per hour. The hand rail was frosty and he lost his hold, falling beneath the train. His body was outside the tracks but one leg was across the rail. He swung his leg clear but the journal of one of the rear wheels caught his trousers leg, and he was twisted against the snow bank. With his free foot he managed to kick himself loose from the journal, only to be caught by the rear step. That tossed him around considerably and when he finally fought clear of that he found himself propped up against the snow bank, feet uppermost. But, nothing daunted, he got to his feet, chased the train and caught it."

A particularly exciting event took place in February, 1914 when George W. Campbell, the Roddis manager, was shot by a disgruntled lumberjack in the office at Park Falls. At the climax of a dispute over wages the logger, whose shooting ability must be scored as mediocre, fired four shots from a .38 calibre revolver at Campbell as the latter sat at his desk. Three bullets missed the target completely, while the fourth glanced off the top of the desk and struck Campbell in the abdomen, causing a slight flesh wound. As the gunman stopped to reload, Campbell and the office clerks dashed to the

101

safety of the vault. Campbell's assailant then submitted to arrest quietly, and ultimately was sentenced to a term of twelve years in the state prison at Waupun.

Word of the shooting led to extraordinary, and unfounded, rumors of an attempted lynching, including one report that the gunman already had been hanged from a telegraph pole. The *Herald*, commenting indignantly that "the reader who was not acquainted with the facts would naturally receive the impression that the citizens of Park Falls are a crew of lawless, bloodthirsty ruffians," quoted verbatim extracts from unidentified "city dailies" as follows:

> *"Fearing a lynching, Sheriff Christiansen of Phillips is on his way to Park Falls and a large force of deputies will be sworn in to protect the prisoner who cowers in his cell listening to the angry threats of the men outside."*

> * * * * * *

> *"Reports from Park Falls Thursday night carried the information that a special train owned by the logging road in that vicinity brought in a number of men who immediately threw a volunteer guard about the jail. An all night guard was kept to prevent any possible outbreak against the prisoner."*

> * * * * * *

> *"According to a report reaching here, the men procured a rope and were upon the point of attacking the man when Campbell, although weak from the wound and excitement, rushed between the men and their intended victim and saved his life."*

But life along the Roddis Line was not always hazardous or burdensome. The wilderness area traversed by the railroad contained many lakes as well as the Chippewa and Flambeau Rivers, and Roddis personnel took full advantage of the fishing and hunting opportunities. There was trout fishing on the Chippewa and bass and muskellunge in the Turtle Lake region. Jack Hobelsberger, a Roddis vice-president, maintained a hunting camp near Island Lake where he regularly acted as host to Roddis customers. Since the area logged by Roddis was almost inaccessible except by rail, there was little fishing or hunting pressure from outsiders, and venison was obtainable so readily that it was referred to in the Roddis family as "Roddis mutton."

"Blueberry Special" trains for the convenience of Park Falls residents were operated occasionally on Sundays in summer. Generally from 75 to 100 patrons showed up, and a train consisting of box cars, flat cars, and a caboose would carry them to choice locations in Iron County where as many as 500 quarts of blueberries would be picked by the group.

The following social item appeared in the *Herald* in September, 1906:

> "*Mrs. G. W. Campbell entertained about twenty-five of her lady friends at an impromptu flat car party Wednesday afternoon. Seats were provided on bales of hay, and the ride in the lovely fresh air out to Agenda and back was greatly enjoyed by every member of this jolliest of parties. There are vague rumors of some of the ladies occupying seats in the front of the car carrying on a passing flirtation with the men working along the right of way, but we can scarcely believe it. Anyway, the men should have no objections.*"

Two photographs of an early morning fire which caused extensive damage to a slide jammer, about 1930. The wooden cab was destroyed completely.

A scene at Camp 7 during the winter of 1924-1925.
Ladders provided handy access for shoveling snow off the roofs.

Snow piled high outside the Camp 7 bunkhouses.

Digging out at Camp 10 after a snowfall.
Holding the shovel is Gust Carlson, the woods superintendent.

It was a chilly, grey winter day during
the early 1930's when engineer Guy Hogan
and brakeman Dan Donner posed at Camp 8
with Engine No. 10, one of the Heislers.

Brakeman Hank Sigman stands next to a loaded car
which has been derailed.

In this scene, dating from about 1930,
efforts apparently are being made to put
a derailed car back on the rails through
the use of ties and a jack.

A wrecked car loaded for a move to Park Falls,
where it will be repaired or scrapped.

At the end of a hunting trip in the fall of 1928,
Roddis personnel climb aboard the caboose.

Roddis train crew with their deer kill at one of the camps.
In the center, left to right, are brakeman Byron Mason, engineer Mert Hayward,
section foreman Bill Martin, and fireman Joe Corrigan.

John A. Morner, Roddis manager at Park Falls (hatless, in front), took a group of high school students for an outing one day in the early 1930's.
The trailer on which they rode was known as the "hay rack" and was pulled by a Model A Ford, known as the "jitney."

Ruth Morner Collection

The Dells Line

7

Immediately to the northwest of the Roddis operations in Iron County there existed, in 1936, practically an entire township of standing hardwood (mostly birch, maple and basswood) and hemlock timber in a quantity exceeding 100,-000,000 feet. This is a hilly region containing, north of O'Brien Lake, the divide between the Mississippi River and Lake Superior drainage systems, and including the foothills of the Penokee Range. Stands of white pine had been cut in the 1890's and driven down the Chippewa and its tributaries, but some pine was still present in less accessible areas.

The forest tract was owned principally by Dells Paper & Pulp Company which operated a paper mill located at Dells Dam on the Chippewa at Eau Claire. From 1929 to 1936 Dells Paper & Pulp's common carrier railroad subsidiary, Delco & Northern Railway Company, connected with the Chicago, St. Paul, Minneapolis & Omaha Railway in Sawyer County west of Park Falls, and ran northward to Hemlock Junction, where it joined Dells' private railroad trackage. Following the exhaustion of local timber supplies, service over the Delco & Northern was terminated in May, 1936, and formal abandonment authority was received from the Public Service Commission of Wisconsin on December 29 of that year.

Early in 1936 Dells Paper & Pulp officials turned their attention to the Iron County holdings. Inability of the Eau Claire mill to utilize hardwoods or hemlock presented a problem, as described by the *Glidden Enterprise:*

111

> *"In logging the large tract of timber northeast of Glidden, Dells Paper & Pulp Co. will have much hardwood which it will have to dispose of to sawmill companies if it does not manufacture itself. In the past it has been difficult to carry on logging operations at certain seasons because of mills refusing to take hardwood logs at certain periods. Hardwood logs are perishable during summer months, and if the company operated its own mill it could cut its hardwood as logged and dispose of surpluses at the most advantageous seasons. Considerable of the hemlock to be logged is not of the standard adapted to paper making and it is expected this will be manufactured into lumber by the Dells Co. if it establishes a sawmill."*

There was some sentiment in the Glidden area for a plan whereby the local taxpayers would purchase the unused Soo Lumber Co. sawmill at Glidden and turn it over to the Dells company in return for assurances that local men would be employed in the mill, thus alleviating the widespread unemployment prevailing during this depressed period. Ultimately this proposal was abandoned.

On February 24, 1936 Dells & Northeastern Railway Company, a wholly owned subsidiary of Dells Paper & Pulp Company, was incorporated as a common carrier. A connection was arranged with the Soo Line at a location in Ashland County known as Sells Spur, about 3½ miles north of Glidden. This locality, site of a small sawmill owned by the Pfiffner Company of Stevens Point, was named after the Sell family, long prominent in the lumber industry in the Glidden area. Because of the presence of Dells & Northeastern Railway and Dells Paper & Pulp Company, Sells Spur became known to many as Dells Spur, with much confusion resulting.

Dells & Northeastern Railway filed with the Public Service Commission, on April 7, 1936, an application for authority to construct, maintain, and operate a common carrier railroad extending approximately 5 miles northeast from Sells Spur to a station in Ashland County to be known as Dryden Creek Junction. The application stated that the railroad was needed to provide a market for "a vast amount

112

of saw logs, pulpwood, and other forest products" in Township 44 North, Range 1 East, bounded by the Chicago & North Western Railway 8 miles to the east, and the Soo Line 4 miles to the north and 5 miles to the west. It was indicated that Dells Paper & Pulp Company would be the principal shipper, although owners of several small tracts were expected to use the line to market their products. The application advised also that Dells & Northeastern would take over the rolling stock and equipment of the Delco & Northern. After a hearing held in Madison on May 11, a certificate of convenience and necessity was granted June 4, 1936.

Meanwhile, an office building, engine house, and machine shop were built at Sells Spur, and more than 30,000 ties were ordered. Rail was obtained from Dells Paper & Pulp Company's private railroad which had connected with the Delco & Northern. By April construction had begun on a set of camps, and arrangements were made with Charles Newell, a Butternut contractor who had been a jobber on the Roddis Line many years before, to grade a right of way for the 5.7 miles common carrier trackage between Sells Spur and Dryden Creek Junction, close to the Iron County line. Beyond Dryden Creek Junction, Dells Paper & Pulp Company built a private logging railroad into its Iron County timber lands. Approximately 3 miles of the private trackage, extending northeast from Dryden Creek Junction to a location known as Camp N, were built on an old railroad grade of the Mellen Lumber Co., which had abandoned the trackage in 1927 and moved its operations to Ontonagon, Michigan.

Beyond Camp N a main line was built to a "Y" approximately 1 mile south of O'Brien Lake. Various branches or spurs radiated from this point to serve landings and camps in the vicinity of Fifteen Lake, O'Brien Lake, Pleasant Lake, and Twin Lakes. A total of approximately 20 miles of private logging railroad ultimately was built beyond Dryden Creek Junction. However, no such quantity was extant at any given time for, as was typical with logging railroads, many of the spurs were of short-lived duration, with the rails being picked up and moved about to new grades from time to time.

On October 13, 1936 the Public Service Commission authorized the commencement of operations by the Dells &

Northeastern, which thus became the last common carrier railroad to be established in Wisconsin. The authorization was issued on a temporary basis because the Commission was not satisfied with certain track clearances at Sells Spur, although conceding that "the track will permit of safe operation for logging purposes." The Commission noted that the line had been ballasted in part with gravel from a local pit and that signs reading "Temporary Railroad" had been erected along each mile of track. Permanent operating authority was granted September 28, 1937, after correction of the clearance problem.

Dells & Northeastern Railway Company was capitalized at $25,000. The Soo Line, its sole railroad connection, made a loan to the D & NE in 1936 which was secured by eight installment notes becoming due each year thereafter in the amount of $1,166.92. The original officers and directors of the railroad corporation, with the exception of the superintendent, held similar positions with Dells Paper & Pulp Company, which owned all stock other than directors' qualifying shares. S. R. Davis, John R. Davis, and E. L. Holden, all of Eau Claire, served as president, vice-president, and secretary-treasurer, respectively, while Robert J. Patrick was assigned local responsibility as superintendent.

The question of how a paper manufacturer at Eau Claire could dispose of timber not suited to its own utilization was answered, in part, by building a small sawmill at Sells Spur to manufacture hemlock lumber for sale on the open market. Some hemlock logs were sold to a mill at Wisconsin Rapids, while pine and hardwood logs also were marketed, with the Roddis veneer plant at Marshfield obtaining much of the hardwood.

By 1943 Dells Paper & Pulp Company had sold the Eau Claire paper mill and was interested in disposing of its Iron County timber and the railroad line. Roddis Lumber & Veneer Company had had nearly five years of experience using truck transportation, in lieu of a railroad, in moving logs from the Island Lake area to Park Falls. Purchase of the Dells Line, which extended to within a mile of the abandoned Roddis grade west of Island Lake, and the Dells timber lands would give Roddis an opportunity to eliminate expensive

114

truck hauls and to obtain substantial new supplies of logs.

An inspection of the Dells Line by Hamilton Roddis satisfied him that, with some rehabilitation, it could be used to advantage in the Roddis operations. On June 1, 1943 Roddis Lumber & Veneer Company bought the entire stock of Dells & Northeastern Railway Company, as well as all of Dells Paper & Pulp Company's timber lands and private railroad in Ashland and Iron Counties. Roddis personnel became officers and directors of the D & NE, with Hamilton Roddis elected president, Louis Korth and William H. Roddis (H.R.'s son) vice-presidents, Mrs. G. A. Seymour secretary, Jack Hobelsberger treasurer, and George Eilenfeldt woods superintendent.

Control by Roddis meant a change in the Dells Line's operating methods. Instead of having a multitude of spurs in the vicinity of each logging camp, Roddis built truck roads to the camps, in some instances picking up existing trackage to provide highway grades. These roads led directly to landings at two places on the Dells Line. One of these was Kirstein's Landing, a very short distance west of Fifteen Lake, while the other, McClaire's Landing, occupying the site of a camp formerly operated by jobber Archie McClaire, was located north of Twin Lakes. Logs were hauled by truck to Kirstein's Landing from Kirstein's Camp, to the east of Pleasant Lake, while McClaire's Landing was the receiving point for logs from Teeters Camp, south of Twin Lakes, which was the terminus of an abandoned Dells Line branch. Some logs also were trucked to the Dells Line from Lipske's Camp, north of O'Brien Lake, but most of the production from that locality was carried to the Roddis mill at Ironwood, Michigan.

The Dells Line maintained service with two train crews. Three steam locomotives, all well aged, were used at various times, with one, No. 5, closing its career as a boiler at the Sells Spur sawmill. Logs and pulpwood were carried either on Soo Line flat cars or D & NE flat cars. A Ford coupe, equipped with rail wheels, which came from the Delco & Northern, accomodated supervisory personnel in traveling over the Dells Line.

Early in 1947 all timber available for shipment over the Dells Line had been cut, and on April 5 the Public Service

115

Commission formally authorized abandonment of the D & NE, barely ten years after the railroad had first commenced operating. Net revenue from railway operations, as reported to the Commission, had ranged from a low of $1,534.50 for 1937, the first complete year, to a high of $5,908.10 for 1944.

Woodrow Kehring

This white building at Sells Spur was the office
of the Dells & Northeastern Railway. It had been converted into
a residence at the time this picture was made, in August, 1970.

Dells & Northeastern No. 102,
a Prairie-type locomotive built
by Baldwin, had seen many previous
years of service as No. 102 of the
West Lumber Co. of Lugerville,
Price County, Wisconsin.

Archie Eineichner, a Dells Line
brakeman, took this picture
in 1941 or 1942, showing engineer
Woodrow Kehring, left, and fireman
Albert Wiedenhoeft perched
rather precariously on top
of No. 102's headlight.

Dells & Northeastern No. 102 and flat cars
loaded with pulpwood. 1941.

A trainload of logs, headed by No. 102, en route to Sells Spur in 1941.

Engine No. 102 performs switching duties
at McClaire's Camp, about 1941.

Dells & Northeastern No. 10 with the line's only caboose,
which had been obtained, second-hand, from the Delco & Northern.

Sleigh hauling in winter along the Dells Line, around 1941.
Leo Heth rides the load, and Archie McClaire, a jobber, and Hank Killinger
stand beside the sleigh.

The photograph above shows a slide jammer
loading birch logs on the Dells Line.

Loading logs on to a Soo flat car, using saplings instead of stakes
to hold the logs in place. This picture is from a moving picture reel
taken by Jack Delaney, a Dells Line fireman, about 1939.

Archie McClaire Collection   *John Delaney Photo, Diane Mihalik Collection*

A McGiffert jammer loading logs
on to a Soo Line flat car.

The steel gang at work on the
Dells Line, about 1939.

A McGiffert jammer and Engine No. 102 at McClaire's Camp. In this picture
the locomotive carries a No. 2 plate, but former Dells Line personnel
insist that No. 102 and No. 2 are the same engine, although the reason for
the apparently temporary use of a No. 2 plate has been forgotten.

Archie McClaire Collection

Tony White, cook for the steel gang,
steps down from the cook car which is parked on the
Teeters Camp branch of the Dells Line.

This view looking backward from
a locomotive cab reveals what
a remarkably narrow right of way
was utilized by the Dells Line.

Engineer Kehring snapped this
photograph of his train of pulpwood,
pulled by No. 102, as it rounded
a curve in 1941 or 1942.

Woodrow Kehring

Woodrow Kehring

Mac McIver, a jobber on the Dells Line, photographed McIver Camp
at O'Brien Lake as it appeared during the winter of 1937.

A glimpse of the Dells Line where it passed close to Camp 3. 1941 or 1942.

Jobber Archie McClaire, who gained much experience in feeding large groups of men as an Army mess sergeant in World War I, prepares a 600-pound hog for the hungry lumberjacks at McClaire's Camp, circa 1940.

Woodrow Kehring   *Archie McClaire Collection*

Archie McClaire, left, and his guests take a Sunday
ride on Archie's own speeder on the Dells Line.
The cabin in the background is the office
of McClaire's Camp and the year is 1939.

Frank Schwilk, who worked as a logger
for Archie McClaire, found time
on weekends to go hunting along the
Dells Line. 1937.

Al Schiller, the cook
at McClaire's Camp, standing
outside the camp kitchen.

No. 102 at Kirstein's Landing in the spring of 1944.
Archie Eineichner, a brakeman, is at the left,
and John Burgmeier, the master mechanic, is in the center.

A Cody jammer loads cars of logs behind No. 102
at Kirstein's Landing in 1944.

Kirstein's Landing in the spring of 1944. In the foreground hemlock logs
are being unloaded from Chester Ball's truck.
During the period the Dells Line was owned by Roddis, Ball
contracted to haul logs from the camps to the landing on the railroad.

Two jammers at Kirstein's Landing with quantities of hemlock
and cedar posts which will be loaded on the Soo Line flat cars.

Appendix

The purpose of this appendix is to offer some assistance to connoisseurs of steam locomotive history. While tracing distinctive features and successive ownerships of locomotives used by railroads which have an unqualified history as common carriers is seldom easy, the burden is much greater in dealing with logging railroads. The latter used second-hand engines almost exclusively, and seldom maintained permanent, detailed motive power records. Nevertheless, with willing assistance from a number of helpful people, an effort has been made to compile separate locomotive rosters for Roddis Lumber & Veneer Company and Dells & Northeastern Railway Company, respectively, as follows:

Roddis Lumber & Veneer Company Locomotives

Road Number	Year Built	Builder & Number	Type	Purchase Date	Disposal
1			4-4-0	1903	Retired about 1911
2nd #1(?)	1909	Lima 2249	Shay	About 1921	
2		Porter	2-6-0		
3		Baldwin	4-6-0	About 1910	
2nd #3	1887	Baldwin 8438	4-4-0	1916	
4	1887	Baldwin 8436	4-4-0	1916	
2nd #4			2-8-0	1936	
5	1923	Heisler 1477	Heisler	About 1925	
6			2-8-0	About 1922	
7	1881	Baldwin 5931	4-4-0	About 1917	Scrapped 1928
2nd #7	1912	Baldwin 39005	2-6-2	1927	Sold to Dells & NE
9?	1899	Lima 632	Shay	1930	
10	1927	Heisler 1551	Heisler	1927	

Notes as to previous ownerships:

2nd. No. 1 originally belonged to Rice Lake Lumber Co., Draper, Wis., then Park Falls
    Lumber Co., Park Falls, Wis., then Hines Hardwood & Hemlock No. 1, Park Falls.
No. 2 bore, on its cab, traces of the initials "G. W. P. Co."
2nd. No. 3 is believed to have been Wisconsin Central No. 101, then Soo Line No. 2034.
No. 4 is believed to have been Wisconsin Central No. 99, then Soo Line No. 2032.
2nd. No. 4 was obtained from Flambeau River Lumber Co., Ladysmith, Wis.
No. 5 was obtained from Bissell Lumber Co., Ladysmith, Wis.
No. 7 was Chicago, St. Paul Minneapolis & Omaha No. 68, then Bayfield Transfer Co.
    and Wachsmuth Lumber Co., Bayfield, Wis.
2nd. No. 7 originally was St. Croix Timber Co. No. 1, Douglas County, Wis., then Mellen
    Lumber Co. No. 7, Glidden, Wis.
No. 9 originally belonged to Alexander & Edgar Lumber Co., Iron River, Wis., later
    Foster-Latimer Lumber Co., Mellen, Wis.

Herb Hollinger, the engineer assigned to No. 7 during the
middle 1920's, became quite attached to this locomotive, and
wrote a poem about it. Inasmuch as the poem contains inter-
esting details of No. 7's history, it seems appropriate for it to
be set out here:

> As I sit alone on the round house track
> My fire is burning low.
> I think of the days that are past and gone,
> The days of long ago.
>
> It was back in 1881
> When from the shops I came
> I was taken out for a trial bout,
> Then placed in the railroad game.
>
> Some locomotives were given a name
> But as I was up-to-date,
> To me was given a number
> It was number 68.
>
> I was built for passenger service
> I was sold to the Omaha.
> I have hauled about a million Swedes
> Who could say nothing else but "yaw."
>
> I hauled fishermen in the Springtime
> And hunters in the Fall.
> And men from many nations
> From Duluth down to St. Paul.

132

There were Irish who came from Ireland
And French who came from France
And Scotch who came from Scotland
Who wore skirts instead of pants.

But as the heavy loads increased
And the population grew,
They found I was not large enough
To haul the fast trains through.

So they took me off the main line
And put me on a branch
Where I was busy hauling farmers
From the city to their ranch.

But as my boiler getting weak
I could not pull the load
I was taken off the branch line
And sold to a logging road.

I landed up at Bayfield
You know that little town
That's where they catch the lake trout
Also the German Brown.

There I was quite happy
I rambled night and day
A hauling logs from out the woods
Down to Chequamegon Bay.

At last one day my job was done
My hogger in new overalls
Took me out upon the Soo Line
And I landed in Park Falls.

Down there I sure was busy
A plowing out the snow
As I rambled up the main line
I sure did like to go.

My hogger was Herb Hollinger
And a likely lad was he
With his hand upon the throttle
While we made for Whiteside Hill.

But now old age is coming
I feel my time is near
I will soon be put on pension
On a siding in the clear.

No more will my fire box brightly glow
As I sit in the summer sun
With rust a gathering on my stack
I have taken my last run.

So now, as times are changing
And I have made my will
They may cut me up for scrap iron
On the rip track on the hill.

Dells & Northeastern Railway Locomotives

Road Number	Year Built	Builder & Number	Type	Purchase Date	Disposal
5			4-6-0	1936	Boiler used in sawmill—about 1940
10	1912	Baldwin 39005	2-6-2	About 1938	Scrapped 1947
102	1916	Baldwin 43339	2-6-2	1936	Scrapped 1947

Notes as to previous ownerships:

No. 5 probably belonged to the Delco & Northern at the time of its acquisition by Dells & Northeastern. Previous ownerships are uncertain, but various clues suggest previous owners might include Duluth & Northern Minnesota Railroad, Knife River, Minn., and Kaiser Lumber Co., Winter, Wis.

No. 10 apparently was previously Roddis 2nd. No. 7 (see Roddis roster and notes). Nevertheless, while this locomotive was in use on the Dells & NE it carried an inspection card of the Rainy Lake Lumber Co., Virginia, Minn.

No. 102 originally was No. 102 of West Lumber Co., Lugerville, Wis., from which company the locomotive was acquired by the Dells & NE. For reasons now forgotten, this engine was identified as No. 2 for a portion of its service on the Dells & NE.

Roddis engine No. 1, in 1910, with a great quantity of hardwood, hemlock and pine logs. Standing at left is Byron Mason, a camp foreman and later a brakeman.

Engine No. 2 as it appeared in 1925. Note the foraging hog behind the tender.

One of two Roddis engines to be designated No. 3 is shown with its crew, consisting of, left to right, fireman Joe Corrigan, engineer Mert Hayward, and brakeman Byron Mason.

The second No. 3 is shown at work in the woods, around 1920, with brakeman Byron Mason, fireman Bill Martin, and engineer Mert Hayward watching the photographer.

The second No. 4 engine, shown here at Park Falls, was already well-aged when it was acquired by Roddis in 1936 from Flambeau River Lumber Co.

May Nelson Collection   *Harvey Huston Collection*

Harold Van Horn Photo, Robert M. Hanft Collection

No. 5, the older of the two Roddis Heislers, at Park Falls.

Engine No. 6 on a woods spur in 1925.

The first No. 7 engine with the water car, circa 1925.

Roddis second No. 7, a 1912 Baldwin, as it appeared when new as No. 1 of the St. Croix Timber Company in Douglas County, Wisconsin.

No. 10 and the second No. 7 at Camp 8 in the early 1930's. In the center is John A. Morner and at right, Con Olson, Roddis manager and assistant manager, respectively, at Park Falls.

Howard Peddle Collection   *J. Arnold Morner Collection*

August Reichert Collection

No. 10, which was apparently the only locomotive purchased new by Roddis, is shown here with a slide jammer picking up logs along the Flambeau River a few miles from Park Falls, around 1930.

A 1925 view of the Chevrolet "business car."

This awesome looking vehicle was a gasoline powered speeder enclosed for winter operation. It was used regularly by the woods superintendent in making his rounds, and came in handy for running errands between Park Falls and the camps.

The Ford automobile, commonly referred to as the "jitney," is shown during the early 1930's at Camp 10 with, from left to right, Anna May Zoesch, Ruth Morner (John A.'s daughter) and the camp blacksmith.

A typical Roddis speeder, at Camp 7.

Engine No. 5 was used by the Dells & Northeastern
only a few short years before it was cut up and its boiler
installed in the sawmill at Sells Spur.

Dells & Northeastern No. 102, which originally was West Lumber Co. No. 102, at Sells Spur on October 16, 1946.

Dells & Northeastern No. 10 pulls empty flat cars into the woods, around 1939. This is believed to be the same locomotive which saw previous service as Roddis second No. 7.

The Dells & Northeastern's "business car," a Model A Ford coupe pictured in 1939, had seen service previously with the Delco & Northern, another Wisconsin short line which also was a subsidiary of Dells Paper & Pulp Co., the original owner of the Dells & Northeastern.

Acknowledgements/Bibliography

A very large measure of gratitude is owed to a long list of generous people.

Especially helpful in the preparation of this book were Mrs. Mary Roddis Connor of Wausau, Wisconsin, a daughter of Hamilton Roddis, and her husband, Gordon R. Connor, who was Roddis manager at Park Falls in 1936 and 1937. In addition to supplying a large quantity of historical data and many photographs, they furnished leads to several fruitful sources of additional material.

Arthur Johnson of Park Falls, Wisconsin, who has been employed by the Roddis and Weyerhaeuser companies since 1927 in a great variety of positions, including service as Camp Clerk at old Camp 15, was most energetic in collecting photographs and maps, putting the author in touch with other helpful former Roddis or Dells personnel, and correcting errors which appeared in the first draft of the manuscript. Many of the more significant photographs in the book appear only because Art Johnson almost literally rescued the originals from the furnace when most of the Roddis records and memorabilia were being destroyed at the time of the merger into Weyerhaeuser.

James P. Kaysen of Cedarburg, Wisconsin, author of *Railroads of Wisconsin, 1827–1937,* shared generously his extensive knowledge of Wisconsin logging railroads. His contributions to the preparation of the map of the Roddis and Dells railroad lines were particularly significant.

Arthur LaBerge of Stetsonville, Wisconsin, who went to work as a top loader and relief jammer operator along the Roddis Line in 1913, provided the author a conducted tour, fifty-seven years later, of large portions of the old Roddis right of way and camp sites, resolving many doubts as to specific locations. His sharp recollections also enabled him to supply answers to a multitude of questions and to identify locale and people in many of the photographs which appear in this volume.

143

Howard Peddle of South Range, Wisconsin was most helpful in tracking down obscure photographs of railroad operations on both the Roddis Line and the Dells Line. Additionally, without his assistance the locomotive data in the Appendix would have been much sparser.

William H. Roddis of Milwaukee, Wisconsin, the son of Hamilton Roddis, lent rare photographs from his father's collection and patiently provided answers to many questions about the operations of the Roddis companies, which he served in various official capacities.

Frank E. Salonen of Minocqua, Wisconsin, who was Camp Clerk at Camps 6 and 7 from 1923 to 1925, made an especially comprehensive photographic record of Roddis' railroad and woods operations during those years. Fortunately, the great majority of his original negatives have been preserved, and his ample descriptions of the details of the scenes shown have fully justified the inclusion of a large number of these outstanding photographs.

Walter E. Scott, Assistant to the Secretary of the Wisconsin State Department of Natural Resources at Madison, in providing copies of the excellent Roddis Line photographs in the Department's collection first made the author of this work aware of the great pictorial potential that would be possessed by a history of this logging railroad. Thus in a large measure he encouraged the publication of this book.

For assistance in providing photographs, historical data, map information, or a combination of the foregoing, the author wishes to express his thanks to the following:

Walter J. Bender, Superior, Wisconsin.
Gerald M. Best, Beverly Hills, California.
Jerome W. Best, Park Falls, Wisconsin.
Lester Blanchard, Park Falls, Wisconsin, son of Frank Blanchard,
    Roddis teamster and barn boss.
John Burgmeier, Park Falls, Wisconsin, former Dells Line master mechanic,
George A. Corrigan, Hurley, Wisconsin, former jobber for Roddis.
Clarence Danckwardt, Butternut, Wisconsin.
Walter W. Dwyer, Chief, Section of Reference Services, Interstate
    Commerce Commission, Washington, D. C.
Robert M. Hanft, Paradise, California.
Miss Josephine L. Harper, Manuscripts Curator, State Historical
    Society of Wisconsin, Madison.
Jack Hobelsberger, Marshfield, Wisconsin,
    a former Roddis vice president who started his Roddis career in 1920.
Jack M. Holst, Portland, Oregon.
Miss Ondre Huston, Winnetka, Illinois.
Keith Jesse, Mercer, Wisconsin, former Roddis locomotive fireman.
Jerome W. Johnson, Whitewater, Wisconsin.
Woodrow Kehring, Glidden, Wisconsin, former Dells locomotive engineer.
Frank Kleinsteiber, Butternut, Wisconsin.
Michael Koch, Scarsdale, New York.
Louis Korth, Hewitt, Wisconsin, who went to work for Roddis in 1908
    and retired as vice president of Roddis Plywood Corporation in 1956.
Leonard Kuehl, Park Falls, Wisconsin.
James W. Lydon, Minneapolis, Minnesota.
Roger Martin, Park Falls, Wisconsin, son of William M. Martin,
    who was employed by Roddis as section hand, section foreman,
    and locomotive fireman and engineer.
Archie McClaire, Sr., Glidden, Wisconsin,
    former jobber on the Dells Line.
M. C. McIver, Mellen, Wisconsin, former jobber on the Dells Line.
Mrs. Diane Mihalik, Proctor, Minnesota, daughter of John Delaney,
    a Dells Line locomotive fireman and engineer.
J. Arnold Morner, Ironwood, Michigan, who was employed by Roddis
    as a pulpwood checker.
Miss Ruth Morner, Minneapolis, Minnesota, daughter of John A. Morner,
    Roddis manager at Park Falls.
Miss May Nelson, Park Falls, Wisconsin.
Oscar M. Nelson, Ogema, Wisconsin, who was foreman at several
    of the Roddis camps.
P. E. Percy, Lima, Ohio.
A. R. Rabbideau, Ironwood, Michigan.

145

August Reichert, Rhinelander, Wisconsin, who was a Roddis jammer
operator.
Otto Schultz, Park Falls, Wisconsin, former Roddis section foreman.
George Steiger, Wakefield, Michigan, former Roddis locomotive engineer.
George Watson, Marshfield, Wisconsin.
Earl Yankee, Rhinelander, Wisconsin, former Roddis brakeman.

Frederick I. Olson, Professor of History at the University of Wisconsin-
Milwaukee, read the manuscript and made many helpful suggestions.

The following specific references were used:

BOOKS:

Andreas, A. T.:
History of Northern Wisconsin.
Western Historical Co., Chicago, 1881.

Curtis, John T.:
The Vegetation of Wisconsin.
University of Wisconsin Press, Madison, 1959.

Fries, Robert F.:
Empire in Pine.
State Historical Society of Wisconsin, Madison, 1951.

Gates, Paul Wallace:
The Wisconsin Pine Lands of Cornell University.
State Historical Society of Wisconsin, Madison, (reprint) 1965.

Hotchkiss, George W.:
History of the Lumber and Forest Industry of the Northwest.
George W. Hotchkiss Co., Chicago, 1898.

Huston, Harvey:
Thunder Lake Narrow Gauge.
Harvey Huston, Winnetka, Ill., 1961.

Interstate Commerce Commission:
Statistics of Railways in the United States.
Government Printing Office, Washington, 1908–1938.

Jones, George O., McVean, Norman S., and others:
History of Wood County, Wisconsin.
H. C. Cooper, Jr. Co., Minneapolis and Winona, Minn., 1923.

Kaysen, James P.:
The Railroads of Wisconsin, 1827–1937.
Railway & Locomotive Historical Society, Boston, 1937.

Koch, Michael:
The Shay Locomotive.
World Press, Inc., Denver, 1971.

Martin, Roy L.:
History of the Wisconsin Central.
Railway & Locomotive Historical Society, Boston, 1941.

Moody's
Analysis of Investments-Industrial Securities.
Moody's Investors Service, New York, 1925–1930.

Moody's
Manual of Investments-Industrial Securities.
Moody's Investors Service, New York, 1952–1960.

Poor's
Manual of the Railroads of the United States.
Poor's Railroad Manual Co., New York, 1908–1940.

Raney, William Francis:
Wisconsin, A Story of Progress.
Perin Press, Appleton, Wis., (revised edition) 1963.

Rector, William Gerald:
Log Transportation in the Lake States Lumber Industry, 1840–1918.
Arthur H. Clark Co., Glendale, Cal., 1953.

Reynolds, A. R.:
The Daniel Shaw Lumber Company.
New York University Press, New York, 1957.

Sorden, L. G.:
Lumberjack Lingo.
Wisconsin House, Inc., Spring Green, Wis., 1969.

Wyman, Walker D.:
The Lumberjack Frontier.
University of Nebraska Press, Lincoln, 1969.

ARTICLES:

Best, Jerome W.:
"Lumberjack Legacy."
Wisconsin Conservation Bulletin, May–June, 1970 (vol. 35, no. 3).

Lydon James W.:
"Park Falls, Wisconsin."
The Soo-Liner, September–October, 1951 (vol. 1, no. 6).

Moran, Joe A.:
"When the Chippewa Forks Were Driving Streams."
Wisconsin Magazine of History, June, 1943 (vol. 26, no. 4).

NEWSPAPERS:

Glidden Enterprise, 1936–1947 (microfilm file at State Historical Society of Wisconsin, Madison).

Marshfield News, various dates.

Marshfield News-Herald, especially Wood County Centennial Edition, August 5–11, 1956.

Milwaukee Journal, various dates.

Northern Photo News (Park Falls), March 2 and March 9, 1950.

Park Falls Herald, 1903–1939 (files at MacGregor Litho, Inc., Park Falls, and at State Historical Society of Wisconsin, Madison).

PUBLIC DOCUMENTS:

Annual Reports of Dells & Northeastern Railway to Public Service Commission of Wisconsin.

Annual reports of Roddis Lumber & Veneer Co. to Wisconsin Railroad Commissioner, Wisconsin Railroad Commission, and Public Service Commission of Wisconsin.

Public Service Commission of Wisconsin case reports.

Wisconsin Department of State corporate records.

Wisconsin Railroad Appraisal of 1904.

Wisconsin Railroad Commission annual reports and case reports.

Printed and bound by

The Lakeside Press, R. R. Donnelley & Sons Company

Chicago, Illinois and Crawfordsville, Indiana

The map was drawn by Donald J. Moody

Design and type styling by Dan E. Smith